What is Existentialism?
~~~~~~~~

Volume I:
History & Principles

by

Frank Scalambrino

Castalia, OH: Magister Ludi Press
MMXXI

What is Existentialism? Volume I: History & Principles
Copyright © 2021 Frank Scalambrino.
Magister Ludi Press is an imprint of the Academic Freedom, Fairness, and Merit-Based Publishing Group (AFF&MBPG).

Frank Scalambrino asserts his moral right to be identified as the author of this publication. Except in those cases expressly determined by law all rights reserved.

Castalia, OH: Magister Ludi Press.
Scalambrino, Frank
ISBN: 978-1947674271 (Paperback)
ISBN: 978-1947674288 (Ebook)
1. Existentialism – Philosophy
2. The Continental Tradition - Philosophy
3. Kierkegaard, Nietzsche, Heidegger, Sartre, Marcel
4. Existentialism – Genealogy
5. Transcendental Philosophy

13 12 11 10 9 8 7 6 5 4 3
Book Cover Picture: (CC BY-SA) 1835 Julius von Leypold. *Wanderer im Sturm* [Wanderer in the Storm]. Public Domain.
(https://commons.wikimedia.org)
Back Cover Picture 2: © 2021 Frank Scalambrino.

Cover design by Frank Scalambrino.

I remember the joy I would experience
at finding some bit of philosophy in a book
that answered some question I had been researching.
I dedicate this two-volume set
to doing that for you.

Table of Contents

Acknowledgements	ix
Volume I Preface	xi
Introduction	
§1 Why is the Question "What is Existentialism?" so Difficult to Answer?	1
§2 How to Understand the Meaning of "Existentialism," Despite so Much Disagreement Among the "Existentialists"	3
§3 On the Origin of the Terms "Existentialist" and "Existentialism"	6
§4 How This Book Is Organized	8
§5 What Is the Difference between Philosophical Archaeology and Philosophical Genealogy?	9
§6 The Necessary and Sufficient Conditions for Existentialism	12
§7 The Seven Principles of Existentialism	13
Philosophy Part I:	
Chapter 1. The "Philosophical Archaeology" Answer:	
Kant's Copernican Revolution	
§0 Overview of Chapter 1	17
§1 To What Does the Word "Existence" Refer?	18
§2 What Does the *Critique of Pure Reason* Teach Us About the Difference Between Consciousness and Existence?	21
§3 What is "Transcendental Philosophy," and How Does It Relate to Consciousness?	25

§4 What Is the "Transcendental Unity of Apperception"? How Does It Relate to Existence? And, How Do Its Constitutional Elements (Origin, Unity, Spontaneous Act) Correspond to the Principles of Existentialism (Mystery, Mineness, Freedom)? 26

§5 The Three Genera with which to Thematize Transcendental Apperception 34

History of Philosophy Part I:
Chapter 2. The "Historical Emergence of Existentialism as a Philosophical Theme" Answer:
Existentialism as the Phoenix of Romanticism

§0 Overview of Chapter 2 41

§1 Existence as a Naturally-Creative Power: Meaning-Making and Life as a Work of Art 42

§2 The Wanderer in the Storm & the Wanderer and Its Shadow 46

§3 From the Mourning of the Future to the Dawning of Eternity: The Truth of Undying Love and Alienation as the Cost of the Freedom to Witness the Future of Your Spiritual Self 48

§4 *Amor Fati*: The Joyful Quest 51

History of Philosophy Part II:
Chapter 3. The "Philosophical Genealogy" Answer:
From Germany to France: Schelling, Schopenhauer, Kierkegaard, Nietzsche, Heidegger, Sartre, and Marcel

§0 Overview of Chapter 3 59

§1 Existentialism against Hegel's Resurrection of Enlightenment Rationalism's Nihilisms: the Nihilism of Being-as-History and the Nihilism of Being-as-Speculative-System 60

§2 Schelling's Positive Philosophy & Schopenhauer's Philosophy of Life 65

§3 Kierkegaard, *The Sickness Unto Death*: The Leap of Faith to Become Who You Are   73
   {1} the major interpretations of Søren Kierkegaard's philosophizing
   {2} Kierkegaard's characterization of the principles of existentialism
   {3} Kierkegaard on worldliness, self-actualization, and the inauthentic as "the demonic"
   {4} Kierkegaard on death and the Knight of Faith

§4 Nietzsche, *Twilight of the Idols*: The Fatal Joy of Existing   81
   {1} the phases of Nietzsche's philosophizing
   {2} Nietzsche's characterization of the constitutional principles of existentialism
   {3} Nietzsche's characterization of the actualization principles of existentialism
   {4} Nietzsche's criticism of the concept of consciousness
   {5} Nietzsche on integrity, sincerity, and the "free death"

§5 Heidegger, *Being & Time*: Be-ing in the Clearing of Care Thrown at Death   99
   {1} The phases of Heidegger's philosophizing
   {2} Heidegger's early phase work: his clarification of Kant's critique of Descartes
   {3} paraphrase of Heidegger's existential philosophy (a vocabulary primer)
   {4} Heidegger's characterization of the constitutional and actualization principles of existentialism in *Being & Time*

§6 Sartre, *Being & Nothingness*: Apparitional Consciousness, Existential Meaninglessness, and *from* Willing as Valuating *to* Responsibility to Subjectivity   119
   {1} the phases of Sartre's philosophizing

{2} a statement of the Cartesianisms and Hegelianisms which plague the constitutional principles of Sartre's existential philosophy

{3} Sartre's characterization of the For-itself as an apparitional consciousness constituting the existing subject

{4} Sartre's characterization of the For-itself in regard to time and his affirmation of Descartes' *cogito ergo sum*

{5} Sartre's "trinity of lack"

{6} Sartre's characterization of the actualization principles of existentialism

§7 Marcel, *The Mystery of Being*: The Generative Power of Commitment, Authenticity as Participation in a Spiritual Community, and Life as Creative Sacrifice   138

{1} the phases of Gabriel Marcel's philosophizing

{2} the writings examined in this section and Marcel's idea of participation

{3} worldliness, despair, and hope, regarding the existential elements of wholeness and totality

{4} how Marcel's "trinity of fidelity" culminates in creative sacrifice

{5} freedom and the spirit world

{6} Marcel's characterization of the actualization principles of existentialism

Bibliography & Further Readings   156
Index for Volumes I & II   177

Acknowledgements

Thank you for purchasing this two-volume set.

I would like to thank Molly for her exuberant spirit and grace. Certainly, her presence in my life helped me make this two-volume set stronger than it may have otherwise been.

Over the years I have benefited greatly from speaking with many different individuals regarding existentialism. I am grateful for all of those conversations, and I would like to especially thank two individuals.

I would like to thank Dr. Zachary Willcutt for our conversations over the years and his comments on the Gabriel Marcel section in Volume I, Chapter 3.

I would also like to thank Dr. Wilhelm Wurzer (1948-2009). His "swan songs" and his grace in the face of death were truly sublime. On our walks, we often talked about Nietzsche and Heidegger, and he taught me something, indeed, about be-ing-toward-death.

I received no outside funding or sabbatical with which to complete this two-volume set.

Volume I Preface

All in, I have been working on this book for over twenty (20) years. Why did I write this book? Because I believe, despite all the books on "existentialism," that this book needed to be written. It needed to be written because it addresses the question: "What is existentialism?" in a way that cannot be found in any *one* other place, *and it answers the question* with what I sincerely believe to be a valuable and unique constellation of Western philosophy.

When we first encounter, and begin to study, philosophy, the experience may seem like watching puzzle pieces pass before us. Eventually we can begin to remember enough of the pieces to recognize that some pieces belong with other pieces, even if we are not completely certain how they link together.

I have finally gathered and linked together the following pieces of philosophy in a way such that even those casually interested in, or merely beginning to study, philosophy can – I believe – benefit from this select presentation of my research.

Initially, I exerted significant effort to keep this project to one book, to one volume. However, to cover all of the topics needed, more than one book was required.

Pagosa Springs
Colorado, USA.
Winter, 2021.

Introduction

§1 Why is the Question "What is Existentialism?" so Difficult to Answer?

Every book discussing "Existentialism" seems to begin the same way. They all seem to begin by stating that the question "What is existentialism?" can't be answered. They, then, go on to discuss all the standard terms, like "freedom" and "death," and, in the end, also do not answer the question: "What is existentialism?"

If that is the first difficulty one encounters when attempting to understand the meaning of existentialism, then the second difficulty is that when we compare what is standardly considered the existentialism of one philosopher with another, we can identify significant disagreement. Thus, for example, on the surface, Søren Kierkegaard (1813-1855) seems to endorse a philosophy quite different from any philosophy endorsed by Jean-Paul Sartre (1905-1980).

A third difficulty one encounters: how these philosophers characterized their own philosophies. In other words, neither Kierkegaard nor Friedrich Nietzsche (1844-1900) referred to themselves as "existentialists" or endorsed any philosophy named "existentialism." Even more to the point, Martin Heidegger (1889-1976) openly and explicitly disavowed the application of any label such as "existentialist" or "existentialism" to his philosophy, and that is despite the fact that it was *his* work *Being & Time* (1927) that popularized the term "existential" and influenced the "French Existentialists."

This leads directly to the fourth difficulty one encounters when attempting to understand the meaning of existentialism, that is, how the "existentialist" philosophers related to each other's work. The best, in my opinion, example of this is the relation between Heidegger and Sartre. On the one hand, Sartre's *Being & Nothingness* (1943) is almost always counted as one of the great works (the so-called "Bible") of existentialism, and Sartre himself understood his book as intimately related to, and a development of, Heidegger's *Being & Time* (1927). On the other hand, Heidegger wrote his "Letter on Humanism" (1947) to explicitly distance himself from Sartre's understanding of "existentialism," and Heidegger even went so far as to describe Sartre's philosophy as "*Dreck*," that is, "muck/trash."[1]

Though there may be additional difficulties (for example, the sheer difficulty of reading the writings of Heidegger or Sartre), these four (4) difficulties seem to be the most significant for a variety of reasons. To mention just a couple of those reasons here, some portion, or all, of these reasons are the ones most noted by other authors, and these are the difficulties which seem to suggest that perhaps the question "What is existentialism?" can't be answered. However, after over twenty years of working on this question and studying the history of Western philosophy, *this two-volume set finally answers the question.*

---

[1] See Hubert Dreyfus's discussion in Bryan Magee's (1987) *Great Philosophers*, Episode 12, "Husserl, Heidegger & Existentialism."

Introduction

§2 How to Understand the Meaning of "Existentialism," Despite So Much Disagreement Among the "Existentialists"

There are three insights that allow us to understand the meaning of existentialism, despite the difficulties enumerated in the previous section. The first insight is that the question, "What is existentialism?" can be answered in multiple ways. The structure of this set follows this first insight in that each chapter of this two-volume set represents one of the multiple ways the question can be answered.

The second insight is that though all of the answers are equally true, one answer stands as the foundation for all the other answers. Indeed, one answer indicates the condition for the possibility of the articulation of the other answers. Thus, even though the question "What is existentialism?" can be answered in multiple ways and even though "existential" topics or themes may be identified in the work of nearly any Western philosopher, "existentialism," as a philosophical movement, has a definite birthdate in the history of Western philosophy. This birthdate coincides with what I call the "philosophical archaeology" answer to the question "What is existentialism?"

On the one hand, the event by way of which existentialism entered Western philosophy can be identified because it was by way of that event that a method and general framework were standardized; that method and general framework gave birth to existentialism by constituting its groundwork.

On the other hand, though it is possible to retrospectively identify topics or themes in the work of nearly any Western philosopher, it would be technically anachronistic to identify any philosophy prior to the birthdate of existentialism as an "existential philosophy." There are many ways we can illustrate support for the claim of anachronism in such instances, some of which will become clear throughout the discussion found in this two-volume set.

However, for now, suffice to say that only within the framework constituting existentialism, can a philosophy genuinely be an existential philosophy. And, to be clear, the framework first emerged in the history of philosophy with what we are calling here the "archaeological answer" to the question, "What is existentialism?"

So, we may use comments made or thoughts formulated by philosophers prior to the birthdate of the framework to articulate a philosophy in regard to existence. Yet, in order for those comments or thoughts to truly be a part of an existential philosophy, they would need to be articulated in regard to a philosophy rooted in the framework of existentialism, and this framework has a definite birthdate.

The third insight, then, is that the differences across the genuine existential philosophies can be accounted for in three different ways:

(1) Some topics *within* the framework constituting existentialism can be interpreted and developed in multiple ways. Thus, existentialism contains multiple philosophies which differ from one another in how they interpret and develop topics within the framework. For example, this accounts for how Kierkegaard's theism and Sartre's atheism can both be understood as existentialist philosophies.

(2) When interpreting and developing topics within the framework constituting existentialism, some philosophers misinterpret aspects of the framework. For example, what constitutes a misinterpretation or a misunderstanding of a

Introduction

topic, despite its being a part of the framework, is any thematization of a topic that articulates an understanding not supported by the framework. Thus, by far, the most common source of misunderstanding regarding various aspects of the archaeological answer involves René Descartes' (1596-1650) philosophy, that is, the influence of the "Cartesian Legacy" in Western philosophy. Ultimately, using Descartes' philosophy of existence as a point of departure is a misunderstanding because it is not supported by the framework.

What this means is that the birthdate of the framework constituting existentialism manifested in the history of philosophy *after* Descartes. So, in the very least, it is anachronistic to read the framework in terms of Descartes' philosophy. Descartes was simply not aware of the framework. It is just like Aristotle doing the philosophy of physics without the concept of gravity. You can borrow Descartes' terminology and try to map it onto the framework, but the truth is that Descartes was not doing that with his own terminology.

In fact, it was deliberate theorizing *away from* Descartes' *cogito* and his understanding of subjectivity that motivated the wave of continental philosophers in Descartes' wake. Everyone from Kant to the German Romantics to Heidegger took pains to differentiate the articulation of their philosophies away from the philosophy of Descartes.

Notice, then, in this way, two philosophies can be existential philosophies by participating within the framework brought into focus by the archaeological answer, and, yet, differ insofar as one of them thematizes a topic within the framework in a way not supported by the framework. Ultimately, as we will discuss at length below, this is the problem with Sartre's existentialism – it is too Cartesian.

5

(3) Lastly, when interpreting and developing topics in light of the archaeological answer, that is, within the framework of existentialism, some philosophers want to solve problems or articulate philosophies that do not take existence as their primary concern. As we will see, this accounts for the relationship, at the philosophical level, between Romanticism and existentialism. Similarly, this accounts for the fact that Heidegger's philosophy is so important for existentialism, despite the fact that he disavowed the moniker "existentialism."

§3 On the Origin of the Terms "Existentialist" and "Existentialism"

Turns out, not even the origin of the moniker is simple and straightforward. On the one hand, credit goes to Martin Heidegger (1889-1976) for his use of the term "existential," for example, the "existential question of the 'who' of *Da-Sein*" in *Being & Time* (1927). On the other hand, from the consensus among scholars, it was Gabriel Marcel (1889-1973) who first used the term "existentialist" to refer to the philosophy of Jean-Paul Sartre (1905-1980). Complicating matters further, there is disagreement among scholars as to exactly when Marcel first used the term. Some sources say, 1943 in a review of Sartre's *Being & Nothingness*; some say 1945 at a colloquium, and some simply say "in the mid-1940s."[2]

What is more, though Sartre, in turn, used the term, referring to Marcel's philosophy as "Christian Existentialism," Sartre and Simone de Beauvoir (1908-1986) initially rejected the

---

[2] Cf. Hyppolite (1955), de Beauvoir (1963), Fulton (1999), Sartre (2000), Flynn (2006), Joseph and Reynolds (2011), and Wahl (2019).

term, later noting: "our protests were in vain... [so] we took the epithet that everyone used for us and used it for our own purposes." (de Beauvoir, 1963: 38).

Moreover, every credible commentator on existentialism nowadays, of course, counts Søren Kierkegaard (1813-1855) and Friedrich Nietzsche (1844-1900) as "19th-century existentialists," though neither of them ever used the terms or self-applied the moniker. Not to mention, again, that many of the existentialists, Heidegger and Marcel among them, explicitly rejected the moniker.

As a result of all this confusion, Sartre is often, misleadingly, referred to as the "father of existentialism" and Kierkegaard referred to as "the grandfather of existentialism." This is one of the untruths that academia perpetuates.

Per my view, Kant is the true father of existential philosophy in that his philosophy functions as the condition for the possibility of existentialism by providing its methodology and framework.

Not recognizing Kant's transcendental philosophy as the ground of existentialism leads to all sorts of odd attempts by academics to articulate a coherent meaning for existentialism. Or, in most cases, to suggest that there is no coherent meaning for the term. For example, consider the following quote from *The Cambridge Companion to Existentialism*.

> If "existentialism" is defined as what Kierkegaard, Nietzsche, Heidegger, and Sartre have in common, it becomes a word with little if any positive meaning, because they would seem to have little more *in common* than a critical relationship to classical modern philosophy... If, on the other hand, it is defined

as the *totality* of what and how they think, the upshot would be utterly incoherent. (Schacht, 2012: 112).

Yet, what those existentialists have *in common* is that they participate in the Kantian Copernican Revolution. And, it is the structure of the transcendental philosophy as a *totality* that allows us to map the existentialists – along with their differences – regarding "what and how they think."

In fact, approaching existentialism as if it were simply philosophizing about a set of themes, or in terms of some aspect of Heidegger's or Sartre's philosophy (without recognizing Kant's transcendental philosophy as the deepest background to all the existential philosophies) is precisely why the question "What is existentialism?" seems unanswerable.

Now, whereas the previous section discussed how it is possible to answer the question "What is existentialism?" the next section discusses how this two-volume set is organized toward actually answering that question.

§4 How This Two-Volume Set Is Organized

This set is organized based on the three insights discussed in §2 above. That is to say, *on the one hand*, the question "What is existentialism?" can be answered in multiple ways, and each of the chapters in these volumes represents one of the ways. In that regard, it is not necessary to read these volumes linearly.

However, *on the other hand*, Chapter 1 – the "philosophical archaeology" answer – does function as the groundwork for all the other answers. In other words, as I will claim and defend in a number of different ways throughout this

Introduction

two-volume set, Kant's transcendental philosophy is the condition for the possibility of "existentialism."

Thus, the philosophical archaeology answer provides a key for understanding all of the other chapters. As a result, it may be most helpful to read Chapter 1 before skipping around the rest of the volumes. Yet, at the same time, if you find Chapter 1 too difficult to understand (given the intimate relation between all of the different answers to the question "What is existentialism?") the other chapters may be read first to deepen one's later reading of Chapter 1. Having organized the chapters into either a primarily philosophical or a primarily historical response to the question should also help orient readers.

Lastly, at the end of this two-volume set readers will find a number of appendices. Methodologically, existentialism is often characterized as concerned with experience and the "concrete," as opposed to the abstract; thematically, as concerned with the finitude of mortality, that is, time and death. Thus, the appendices discuss the relevance of phenomenology and temporality for existentialism, while addressing a number of important, though miscellaneous, concerns.

§5 What is the Difference between Philosophical Archaeology and Philosophical Genealogy?

As high flown as these technical terms may sound, this distinction is actually simple and straightforward. Both terms contain the ancient Greek *logos*, which, philosophically, means "to give an account of." In regard to the first term, the ancient Greek *archē* refers to "beginning," "origin," "principle," or "source." Hence, the "philosophical archaeology" answer refers to a *philosophical* account of the origin of existentialism.

In this way, I take the philosophical archaeology answer to the question "What is existentialism?" to provide the *philosophical* principle that may be identified as the origin of existentialism, and, as already indicated, I believe the principle of existential philosophy to be Kant's Copernican Revolution. This is expressed in a number of different ways throughout. For example, Kant's transcendental philosophy is the groundwork, the framework and methodology, or the "condition for the possibility" of existentialism, and so on.

The ancient Greek *genos*, in "genealogy," refers to "family" in the sense of "family resemblance" or "lineage of kinship." So, philosophical genealogy refers to the historical account of the origin of existentialism. That is to say, it provides an account of the *historical* lineage of philosophies with a family resemblance or lineage of kinship to existentialism. This genealogy is twofold: first in regard to the history of the development of themes from German Romanticism to existentialism and second in regard to the history of the most important philosophical figures associated with existentialism.

It is unique to these books and my approach to the question "What is existentialism?" that I present an answer regarding existentialism's historical lineage invoking the German Romantics Hölderlin, Schelling, Novalis, and Schopenhauer.[3] Moreover, it may seem odd to some readers that the name Schopenhauer appears among the German Romantics; however, I follow and agree with Nietzsche here that

---

[3] Cf. Frank Scalambrino, "The Continental Tradition" In *The Philosophy of Being in the Analytic, Continental, and Thomistic Traditions*. London: Bloomsbury, 2020.

Introduction

Schopenhauer's philosophy should be understood as a "pessimistic Romanticism." Thus, by way of a philosophical-historical lineage, Chapter 2 reveals the roots of existentialism to include the themes and figures of German Romanticism.

Lastly, Chapter 3 provides the second part of the *historical* lineage of existentialism by way of the *primary figures* constituting the "philosophical genealogy" answer. These figures, then, span from the positive philosophy of Schelling and the philosophy of life of Schopenhauer across the standard existentialists to include the "French Existentialists." Yet, *on the one hand*, there are philosophers considered, by some, to be "existentialists" whom I will not discuss here. I have made this choice because they are not essential enough to existentialism, per my view, to make their inclusion here necessary.

On the other hand, what Chapter 3 does include is a discussion of the polemic against Hegel's philosophy, which I do consider necessary for readers to understand, since, otherwise, if we were to merely regard the history of existentialism from a chronological point of view, it may appear convoluted. That is to say, Hegel's philosophy, despite taking Kant's philosophy as a point of departure, imported a number of pre-Kantian understandings into the historical lineage of the scholarship moving from Kant to existentialism. Though this can only be mentioned here given the complexity of its truth, it will be sufficiently discussed in §1 of Chapter 3.

§6 The Necessary and Sufficient Conditions for Existentialism

Though having four sides is a *necessary* condition for a shape to be a square, having four sides is not a *sufficient* condition, since a shape could have four sides and be a rectangle. However, a shape cannot be a square, unless it has four sides; therefore, having four sides is a necessary condition for a shape to be a square. At the same time, the set of necessary conditions for a shape to be a square, when taken together, constitute the sufficient condition*s* for a shape to be a square.

Thus, on the one hand, (a) participation in Kant's Copernican Revolution is the **necessary condition** for existentialism. It is the necessary condition for a philosophy to truly be an existential philosophy. On the other hand, (b) there are a set of topics and themes which function as the **sufficient conditions** for participating in the philosophy of existentialism. In other words, taking a position regarding *the set* of topics and themes functions as sufficient for a philosophy to truly be an existential philosophy.

To be clear, consider how these conditions relate to one another:
- Though it is possible to address (b) the topics and themes by denying their importance or refusing to articulate a philosophy in regard to them, if a philosophy addresses the topics and themes by acknowledging their importance and if a philosophy is articulated by taking positions in regard to them, then that philosophy is an existential philosophy.

Introduction

- However, it is not possible for a philosophy to address the topics and themes by acknowledging their importance and it is not possible for a philosophy to be articulated by taking positions in regard to them, *unless* (a) that philosophy participates in transcendental philosophy. That is to say, the philosophy would need to participate in Kant's Copernican Revolution.

Yet, insofar as transcendental philosophy can be developed into non-existential philosophies, participation in Kant's Copernican Revolution is not a sufficient condition for existentialism. In sum, the Copernican Revolution and the seven (7) principles are the necessary and sufficient conditions for existentialism.

It is in this way that the "philosophical archaeology" answer – stated in Chapter 1 below – discusses the seven (7) principles of existentialism from which the topics and themes (which we just indicated as sufficient for existentialism) directly stem. Thus, taking any position other than merely negating the themes and topics that constitute the sufficient conditions for existentialism requires one to accept the Kantian Copernican Revolution and articulate a philosophy within the framework of transcendental philosophy. For, Kant's transcendental philosophy is the condition for the possibility of articulating a philosophy stemming from the principles of existentialism.

§7 The Seven Principles of Existentialism

In §5 above, I pointed out that the archaeological answer to the question "What is existentialism?" unearths the original principles that constitute existentialism. After writing the philosophical archaeology answer, that is, after writing Chapter 1 of this book, it became possible for me to enumerate and state the principles of existentialism. Thus, I have identified the following seven (7) principles. Transcendental philosophy is the ground of these principles, and it is as if they are seeds in that ground from which *all* the topics and themes of existentialism stem.

The seven (7) principles are:
> {*The Constitutional Principles*}
> 1) Mystery, or Existence Exceeds Consciousness;
> 2) Freedom, or Meaning-Making (Freedom to Determine & Understand One's Own Life);
> 3) Mineness, or the Mineness of Existence over Worldliness;
> 4) Anxiety, or Conscience and Care (this is the inverse of the *scala amoris* from Plato);
>
> {*The Actualization Principles*}
> 5) Authenticity, or Be-ing-in-the-World;
> 6) Integrity, or the Resolute Be-ing-in-Time of Commitment;
> 7) Sincerity, or Be-ing-toward-Death.

Whereas principles 1-3 & 6 all come from Kant's *Critique of Pure Reason*, principle 4 comes from his *Critique of Practical Reason*, his *The Metaphysics of Morals*, and his *Religion Within the Limits of Reason Alone*. Principles 6 & 7 can be found in both Kant's *Critique of Pure Reason* and his *Religion Within the Limits of Reason Alone*. These principles are discussed more thoroughly in the following chapters.

What is Existentialism?

Volume I:
History & Principles

Philosophy Part I:
Chapter 1. The "Philosophical Archaeology" Answer: Kant's Copernican Revolution

> "Existence is not at all discussed in logic – rather what is discussed is not how a thing is the ground of other things, but how a concept is the ground of other concepts... We now want to consider the possibility of a real ground... not simply a logical one... When the thing which is to be inferred is *really* distinguished from the other, then no human reason can comprehend the possibility that one thing could be the ground of another thing, experience teaches it, but reason cannot make it conceivable to us."
> ~Immanuel Kant, *Lectures on Metaphysics*, (29:809).

§0 Overview of Chapter 1

The purpose of this chapter – Chapter 1 – is to provide the "philosophical archaeology" answer to the question "What is existentialism?" As the Introduction has already made clear, the philosophical archaeology answer takes Kant's Copernican Revolution, that is, his transcendental philosophy, as its point of departure. In order to provide this answer, then, the chapter has been divided into five sections, and, all together, these sections provide a statement of the principles of existentialism.

The first section explains to what the term "existence" refers, and in order to accomplish this it enters into a discussion of the meaning of the term "reality." Section Two builds off of Section One by explaining how to understand the relation between consciousness and existence within the context of transcendental philosophy. Thus, Section Two ends by reminding us how to think about Kant's Copernican Revolution.

Section Three picks up from where Section Two left off by clarifying that transcendental philosophy is a philosophy that employs the transcendental method, which is to say that it takes Kant's Copernican Revolution as its point of departure; thus, transcendental philosophy refers to a philosophy of the capacities which constitute our awareness of be-ing-in-time and a philosophy which brings the transcendental point of view regarding experience into focus.

Finally, the first three sections culminate in the fourth and fifth sections. Section Four initiates the discussion regarding the principles of self-actualization, while clarifying the constitutional principles. Section Five clarifies the meaning of the principles of self-actualization. Thus, Section Five provides a list of the seven principles of existentialism, concluding Chapter 1's articulation of the philosophical archaeology answer to the question "What is existentialism?"

§1 To What Does the Word "Existence" Refer?

In transcendental philosophy, the word "reality" means "mind external." The reason it means mind external is because there is a difference between reality and the psychological re-presentation of reality. For example, when you read or hear the word "reality" and you ask questions like: "what does it mean?" or "to what does it refer?" all of that activity takes place in your mind.

The *activity* that is happening is real *activity*. In other words, the content of your mind *actually is* mental and *actually is* occurring in time; yet, we need to recognize is that there is a difference between being actual and being mental. Once we recognize this, we can appreciate the value of keeping our focus on *actuality*. Instead of focusing merely on mental constructions that *relate* to actuality, we strive to keep our focus on reality, and to remain mindful of our *contact* with reality.

The "Philosophical Archaeology" Answer

Thus, we have philosophical mantras, so to speak (think Socratic Schools here), that we recite whenever the momentum of general logic gestures toward bewitching our minds and moving our awareness away from contact with reality – making us unmindful of our contact with reality:

"If all I ever have are ideas about food, then, eventually, I will actually starve." There is a difference between the actual food *outside* your mind and the psychological experience you have regarding the food outside your mind.

The food outside your mind has nutritional content, your thoughts do not. The food outside your mind is *real*, the food inside your mind is not. In other words, the food outside your mind actually **exists** in reality. The food inside your mind may be said to exist as mental states, but not as *real* food. Hence:

The reality of your existence is outside your mind.

Yet, even this truth does not stop your mind from processing contact with itself and contact with reality. So, one way we could articulate what we hope to accomplish with mantras of this sort is: To remain mindful of the truth of the mind's reality, it is as if *that mindfulness* gives us a different point of view from which to observe our experience of reality.

Now, that point of view was philosophically explicated by Immanuel Kant (1724-1804). It is called the "transcendental point of view." No matter how similar it may be to some understandings of Buddhism (and it certainly is), it is also the heart of "transcendental philosophy," and transcendental philosophy should be understood as the origin, the proper point of departure, and the proper context – that is to say, the *archē* – of all philosophies that are truly existential.

Notice, then, that though we could create copious lists of philosophers and philosophies that intersect with many of the various aspects of the genus "existential philosophy," credit for explicating the transcendental philosophy as a philosophy and, therefore, allowing it to function as a ground for us, goes to Kant and his Copernican Revolution.

It is, of course, possible to retrospectively and anachronistically use the transcendental point of view to articulate and elaborate aspects of philosophies appearing in history prior to Kant's original enunciation of the transcendental philosophy. For example, Heidegger's readings of Aristotle or my readings of Plato, and so on. However, it would technically be forcing a horizon of meaning onto the writings of those philosophers – a horizon upon which they were not gazing when they articulated their philosophies.

Thus, I consider it wrong to believe Plato was an existentialist; however, I consider it perfectly legitimate to provide an existentialist reading of his philosophy. To do so would be to bring his philosophy into focus by way of the transcendental point of view and, then, to elaborate and develop the topics discussed in his writings insofar as they regard *existence*.

This understanding of the term "existence" as referring to reality divides into a threefold view of the reality of existence. That is, in this way, I can envision the reality of this body, the *existence* of which, I must cope. I can envision the reality of the cosmos, the *existence* of which, I am a part. And, I can recognize that I – that is, to whatever it is that the "I" can refer to truthfully in reality – *am* outside of my mind. I exist outside of my consciousness of my existence: *existence exceeds consciousness*.

The "Philosophical Archaeology" Answer

On the one hand, then, the reality of my *relation* to my mind comes into focus (the relation between my mind and the reality of my existence), and that may be called transcendental psychology. On the other hand, the reality of all that *relates* to my mind from outside it through the senses may be called transcendental cosmology.

When we think of what is necessary in reality, we can begin to remember trustworthy characterizations of the way reality functions, the way it moves. The necessity of the reality to which our minds relate may be called "transcendental theology." For, it is in the heart of one's soul that divinity speaks, it is through the sublime necessity of reality that we wrestle with fate, and it is through the sublime necessity of reality that we witness the mortality of our existence.

Existence *is*, and we are a part of what exists. This is why the first principle of existentialism is mystery. Because existence exceeds consciousness, consciousness cannot contain or fully know existence.

§2 What Does the *Critique of Pure Reason* Teach Us About the Difference Between Consciousness and Existence?

Because that which is conscious is outside of consciousness, it may be true that we cannot become fully conscious of what is outside of consciousness. Of course, Kant understood the transcendental dimension in this way. In other words, there is not only a distinction between that which exists as a thing-in-itself and that thing-as-an-object-for-us; likewise, the existing "thing" that I am, my conscious awareness of it, and my capacity to bring-to-words that existence are all distinct.

I will merely mention in passing that though the term "unconscious" will always have relational meaning, that is, there are things of which we are not conscious, the attempt to formulate a genus of *the* Unconscious is an exercise in pure reason. Such attempts lose sight of the transcendental point of *view* with which we relate to reality. In other words, even if it may be technically correct to say we are somehow unconscious of transcendental reality (since it is outside of the mind), and even if the content of the concepts being used in such attempts are empirical or pertain to bodily existence, such attempts fail to describe be-ing as it actually is. The logic (or lack thereof) with which conclusions regarding conceptions of unconsciousness are drawn remains formal – that is, general, not transcendental – and confined to subjectivity and objectivity.

"[W]e are informed by sophistical physiology that
'the key to the knowledge of conscious mental life
lies in the unconscious.'
But if one cannot explain the transition from unconsciousness
to consciousness, what does this say about the key?"
~Søren Kierkegaard (*Journals and Notebooks, Vol IV*, p. 64)

There are many ways to point out that existence exceeds consciousness. For example, we can follow – what, again, ultimately comes from Kant – the distinction between cosmological time and time-*consciousness*.

The very constitution of individual existing is such that one cannot be conscious of all that exists. The quantitative reason is that reality is too vast for consciousness to enclose, and, qualitatively, the rate of change occurring outside of the mind (in the cosmos) is faster than consciousness can track.

The "Philosophical Archaeology" Answer

In sum, we recognize existence exceeds consciousness by recognizing that consciousness is encapsulated. Consciousness apprehends portions of a cosmological existence which is in such a state of flux that it changes faster than consciousness can change. This doesn't even mention the fact that consciousness has a scope problem; that is to say, (whereas the former point was temporal, this point is "spatial") the mind can only relate to a *portion* of all that exists at any time.

Notice, then, on the one hand, consciousness of my existence as persisting-through-time is actually unable to apprehend the truth, or lack thereof, of the persistence of the *existence* of which I am a part. On the other hand, it is through consciousness that my individuation from existence is reflected. And, of course, I neither exist nor cease to exist dependent upon consciousness. Consciousness, self-consciousness, and even unconsciousness all depend on existence, existence does not depend on consciousness.

Thus, the existence that I am pulses-forth into consciousness, and that pulsing constitutes time-consciousness. For example, we recognize that this is a different moment from a previous moment, and so on. Further, because the transcendental point of view allows for us to become aware of our existence as exceeding consciousness, we can differentiate between the content and the process of that awareness.

In other words, the process by which we come to an awareness that our existence exceeds our consciousness of it is called "transcendental apperception" (discussed in §4 below) and though the capacity of self-consciousness is insufficient to represent the reality of our existence, we can arrive at a deeper understanding of our existence by examining the process through which we experience reality.

The ground of that process may be called "time-consciousness." However, the better term is "temporality" in that this latter term refers directly to the Copernican Revolution. That is to say, since the mind does not conform to mind-external reality but mind-external reality conforms to the mind, time represents the very ground and constituting event of experience.

In the Transcendental Aesthetic of the *Critique of Pure Reason*, Kant called time the "inner sense," and it is technically an intuition, not a concept of the understanding. Therefore, temporality is the better term, since it signals time as the constitutional grounding of experience by the existing individual. This will all make more sense by the end of this chapter; however, for now, the important piece to remember is that as the existence that I am pulses-forth into consciousness, there are two features that allow us to combine all of the pulses of consciousness into a coherent conscious experience of reality.

First, each conscious experience is constituted by being-in-time, and, second, each conscious experience *belongs* to the *reality* of the existing individual. This can be recognized straightforwardly by noticing two features regarding experience: first, all of our conscious experiences are indexed by time and that when we make meaning out of our experiences, what we focus on in any given moment (synchronically) is ultimately a choice. Second, when we construct a narrative regarding moments across time (diachronically) we not only choose what moments to consider in our construction, but we also identify those moments in terms of their index in time. The first feature will now be discussed in the next section, and the second feature, which is called "mineness," will be discussed in §4 below.

The "Philosophical Archaeology" Answer

§3 What Is "Transcendental Philosophy," and How Does It Relate to Being-in-Time?

Recalling the distinction between cosmological time and time-consciousness, specifically the truth that reality exceeds consciousness' capacities to apprehend it, even before it exceeds consciousness' capacities to comprehend it: To be in time is to *be* along a frequency of the cosmos. The insight that different species *experience* cosmological time differently is often stated with time-consciousness as its point of departure; however, it can be stated with the reality of cosmological time as its point of departure. In doing so, we are able to see that the speeds at which some parts of the cosmos change are different from the speeds at which other parts of the cosmos change.

Thus, though entire volumes can be, and have been, written on transcendental philosophy, for the purpose of answering the question: "What is existentialism?" transcendental philosophy also refers to a philosophy of the capacities which constitute our awareness of be-ing-in-time and a philosophy which takes the transcendental point of view as its point of departure.

Of course, transcendental philosophy is transcendental because it employs the transcendental method, which we can equate, for the purpose of this two-volume set, with the logic of Kant's Copernican Revolution. Further, transcendental philosophy is transcendental because it brings the transcendental dimension into focus, and, in terms of the mineness of existence, the "transcendental dimension" refers to the portion of existence that can be brought into awareness through transcendental apperception.

In conclusion, the philosophical archaeology answer to the question "What is existentialism?" is that transcendental philosophy is the condition for the possibility of existentialism. This is why the philosophical archaeology answer is placed as Chapter 1 in this book: transcendental philosophy refers to the requisite paradigm of thought to bring forth *all philosophies that are properly called "existential."*

§4 What Is the "Transcendental Unity of Apperception"? How Does It Relate to Existence? And, How Do Its Constitutional Elements (Origin, Unity, Spontaneous Act) Correspond to the Principles of Existentialism (Mystery, Mineness, Freedom)?

Over the decades, I have come to believe that understanding what Kant meant by "the transcendental unity of apperception" may be the single-most important concept with which to understand existential philosophy. Though the Kant quote that we will examine here may be a bit difficult to read, I believe the explanation found in this section will, ultimately, be sufficiently straightforward for readers interested in existentialism to grasp.

Originally, the term "apperception" was invented by Leibniz, and it means *to perceive yourself perceiving*. And, recall, Kant, in the *Critique of Pure Reason* (A 271/B 327), explicitly articulated his relation to John Locke (1632-1704) and Gottfried Leibniz (1646-1716). The key difference between them and Kant, as we shall see, is that Kant prefaced his use with the term "transcendental." First and foremost, this signals to us that transcendental apperception *differs from both* Empirical and Rationalist apperception.

The passage for us from Kant appears in §16 of his second edition of the Transcendental Deduction section of the *Critique of Pure Reason*. The most relevant parts of this section for us run from its beginning at B 132 to B 134. Given that we

The "Philosophical Archaeology" Answer

are reading this passage from Kant toward articulating an answer to the question "What is existentialism?" the passage will point us toward two other sections in the 2nd Edition Transcendental Deduction, §17 and §25.

One last note of preparation before reading the passage. What Kant has in mind here is that consciousness presents itself in discrete/distinct units across time. What this means is very simple and straightforward. It means that I can easily distinguish that not only is the coffee mug I am experiencing now the same coffee mug I experienced last week, but, also, I can easily distinguish that I am experiencing this coffee mug, now, and not some other object. Similarly, if I turn toward the East wall, then I experience that wall, and I no longer experience the West wall. My consciousness presents that which I am experiencing as *distinct* from my other experiences.

With that in mind, then, how are all these discrete units of consciousness connected? They must be connected for them to all be *mine* (for example, that *I think* them). As we will see, this brings us directly to the concept of mineness, but it also directly confronts us with the problem of "the subject."

For, we could take the Rationalist approach and say that the discrete units of consciousness are connected because they are all units of consciousness. This leads directly to the Rationalist conception of the subject as a non-material substance, and as a mental substance it is understood to be an absolute consciousness.

The Empirical approach would be to suggest that the discrete units are connected to one another through the physical unity of the body, and this leads directly to the Empiricist conception of the subject as the organized physical body and its capacity for memory across time.

Since this section is about Kant's discussion of transcendental apperception, I will not discuss the problems with the Empiricist conception here; rather, that will be discussed below in §8 of the first chapter of Volume II. Suffice to say here, that apperception and its corresponding conception of the subject will be neither that of the Empiricist nor that of the Rationalist. Keeping this in mind will help ward off misunderstandings.

Primed with what was just noted, the following quote from Kant should not be as difficult as it otherwise might be. According to Kant,

> The *I think* must *be able* to accompany all my representations; for otherwise something would be represented in me that could not be thought at all, which is as much as to say that the representation would be either impossible or else at least would be nothing for me. (B 132).

At this point, Kant has stated exactly what the previous five paragraphs clarified. Continuing the quote from Kant,

> That representation that can be given prior to all thinking is called *intuition*. Thus, all manifold of intuition has a necessary relation to the *I think* in the same subject in which this manifold is to be encountered. (Ibid).

There are two pieces to emphasize here. First, Kant is showing us that the consciousness through which I think all these discrete experiences is separate from, but indicates the existence of, "the same subject." In other words, the self-consciousness that manifests indicates both that the discrete units of consciousness are being combined and that the unification of these units involves a unity. The unification points back to the unity of the subject having experiences, and the self-consciousness associated with recognizing the connectedness across the different and discrete experiences.

The most important piece to understand here – and it is the piece that most people miss – is that the "I think" is not the subject. The "I think" is the self-consciousness that can be said to belong to the subject. The "I think" cannot be the subject or the I think would fall back into the exact same problem.

In other words, regarding my discrete conscious experiences, some of those moments – but not all of them – will include self-consciousness. When I look at the West wall it is possible for me to apperceive that I am perceiving the West wall, but I can also perceive the West wall without perceiving that I am perceiving the West wall. I can perceive the West wall without a moment of self-consciousness.

What this means is that when we talk about discrete units of consciousness, moments of self-consciousness fall into the category of units of consciousness. Thus, if self-consciousness and the subject are considered to be the same thing, then we have not solved the problem, rather we would still have the problem that we would not be able to account for how the discrete moments of self-consciousness are connected.

Thus, consciousness and unconsciousness (as should be crystal clear by the end of this set) belong to a different order than existence, and existence is more primordial than consciousness and unconsciousness. Think of it like this: consciousness and unconsciousness can be located in time. There are moments of consciousness and there are moments of unconsciousness. If we call these moments mental states (mental states of consciousness and unconsciousness), then notice that the order of existence is more primordial because mental states depend on existence, but existence does not depend on mental states. Moreover, things like coffee mugs exist and are neither conscious nor unconscious.

Why is all this important? Because we are trying to identify and understand existence. People who are ignorant of existential philosophy tend to misunderstand their existence because they have not thought through the possible conceptions Kant is leading us through here.

Before moving on to the rest of Kant's quote, we want to point to one more word from the last Kant block quote. On the one hand, it is important to understand how Kant visualized what he is discussing above, and looking at this word will help us. On the other hand, looking at this word will provide us with a summary of the ground we just covered.

The word in the block quote just above is "necessary." Kant mentions the "manifold of intuition" which means, in any actual moment of experience we are considering, all of the content of experience which can potentially be made conscious. He says that the manifold has a necessary relation to the "I think." The relation is necessary because the discrete moments of conscious experience can only be connected if there is something that is able to connect them. And, whatever it is that connects them, its *existence* cannot be limited merely to these discrete moments; in other words, whatever it is that connects them must *unify* them. It must *be* the *unity* of them.

Further, his use of the word "necessary" reminds us that this insight is the fruit of the transcendental logic at work in the application of the transcendental method to experience. In other words, Kant is not playing some strange kind of "what if" game here. Kant is telling us that it is necessarily true for each individual: that your existence is more than your consciousness

The "Philosophical Archaeology" Answer

of it, and, though you can become self-conscious, whatever the content of that self-consciousness, self-consciousness and existence are different. It may be helpful to state the same thing this way: If we want to say that existing is be-ing-in-the-world, then be-ing self-conscious and be-ing-in-the-world are different. What is more, you must exist in *order* to be self-conscious, so existence is of a more prime *order* (it is more primordial) than (the order of) self-consciousness.

Moving on to the remainder of the passage from Kant's 2nd Edition Transcendental Deduction, Kant explained,

> But this representation [of the I think] is an act of *spontaneity*, i.e., it cannot be regarded as belonging to sensibility. I call it the *pure apperception*, in order to distinguish it from *empirical* apperception, or [I] also [call it] the *original apperception*, since it is that self-consciousness which ... produces the representation *I think*, which must be able to accompany all other representations and which in all consciousness is one and the same... I also call its unity the transcendental unity of self-consciousness... (B 132).

Notice that Kant is still clarifying why he refers to what he is discussing as "transcendental apperception." There are three elements we need to be sure to understand from this quote.

First, Kant calls the *representation* that an existing individual is the unity of all the discrete moments of conscious experience "an act of spontaneity." This is very important for us. Second, Kant calls it "original apperception," and refers to its "unity" as transcendental unity. Let's take each of these elements one at a time: act, origin, and unity.

In regard to the first element, Kant wanted to emphasize that the "I think" that represents the existing individual who is having a moment of self-consciousness is an act of spontaneity. This is important because it reveals that the act is being performed out of the order of existence and the act is not being caused. It is not being caused by any aspect within the order of mental states (consciousness, self-consciousness and unconsciousness) and it is not merely part of a causal chain of aspects within the order of existence. In other words, the order of existence is free. It performs its *acts* freely. That is to say, *spontaneity evidences existential freedom*.

In regard to origin, that Kant calls the self-consciousness that is the representation of the "I think" (the consciousness that all of these mental states are *mine*), "original apperception" explicitly tells us that it is an apperception of the *origin* of this consciousness. In other words, the self-consciousness that is the becoming-conscious that all of these discrete mental states are mine is an apperception of the origin of *that* self-consciousness. Of course, the *origin* of that self-consciousness is the existing individual.[4]

Recall that apperception means to perceive oneself perceiving. Put another way, we could say that apperception is simultaneously *both* perception *and* the perception that one is perceiving. Thus, we can say: the self-consciousness that is "original apperception" is simultaneously *both* consciousness of the mineness of my conscious states *and* the consciousness of

---

[4] It's worth stressing one more time here that this insight clarifies for us that the existing individual and the existing individual's self-consciousness are different, and the self-consciousness depends on the existing individual in a way that the existing individual does not depend on the self-consciousness.

The "Philosophical Archaeology" Answer

the origin of that self-consciousness. Importantly, becoming-conscious that self-consciousness originates from something does not mean that that origin is consciousness.

Lastly, then, in regard to unity, recall that, on the one hand, discrete conscious states are *necessarily* combined, and, on the other hand, this combination reveals there is the element of unification. In other words, from the origin there is an act of synthesis that apperceptively combines states of consciousness.

Here, then, is Kant's concluding summary statement to the passage we have been examining.

> Therefore, it is only because I can combine a manifold of given representations *in one consciousness* that it is possible for me to represent the *identity of the consciousness in these representations* itself, i.e., the *analytical* unity of apperception is only possible under the presupposition of some *synthetic* one...
>
> only because I can comprehend their manifold in a consciousness do I call them all together *my* representations; for otherwise I would have as multicolored, diverse a self as I have representations of which I am conscious. (B 133-134).

Notice that Kant anchors his revelation of the transcendental unity of apperception in terms of the unity of mineness. What is more, notice the word "comprehend" in his anchoring. This anchoring leads us directly to the next, and final, section of this chapter; that is, the conclusion to the philosophical archaeology answer to the question "What is existentialism?" What we will see is that the points stressed above regarding act and unity are developed in existentialism into the themes of meaning-making and the self-understanding of be-ing-in-the-world, respectively.

To conclude, we should take a moment to make a summary statement of what we should have learned from this very important section. First, transcendental apperception shows us that *that which* **is** *conscious* – the **existing** individual – is outside of consciousness. Second, the constitutional elements of transcendental apperception – origin, unity, and act – correspond to the constitutional principles of existentialism, mystery, mineness, and freedom, respectively.

§5 The Three Genera with which to Thematize Transcendental Apperception

As mentioned in the previous section, in order to provide the archaeological answer to the question "What is existentialism?" the passage from Kant, which we examined regarding the transcendental unity of apperception, points us toward two other sections in his 2nd Edition Transcendental Deduction, §17 and §25. In this concluding section to Chapter 1 and the archaeological answer, then, we will develop the above insights regarding act and unity, respectively.

In regard to the question "What is existentialism?" we may say that Kant's §17 is about meaning-making in general. Kant titled §17, "The principle of the synthetic unity of apperception is the supreme principle of all use of the understanding." Just as consciousness depends on the existing individual, so too understanding is grounded in the existence of the individual. In this way, as Kant made clear, making meaning out of the contents of our conscious experiences depends on an *act* by the existing individual. A simple illustration of this is that we choose to what we pay attention. Thus, in general, this *act* is ultimately produced out of *freedom*. We are free to make meaning out of our experiences in whatever way we will.

Yet, as Kant pointed out in §16, no further representations can be made in regard to the transcendental being revealed through the transcendental unity of apperception. So, how can there be any meaning-making in regard to the existing individual? How are we to *determine* the meaning of existence?

Kant answers this question in §25, and it is worth quoting him at length:

> in the synthetic original unity of apperception, I am conscious of myself not as I appear to myself, nor *as* I am in myself, but only *that* I am... my own existence is indeed not appearance (let alone mere illusion), rather the determination of my existence can only occur in correspondence with the form of inner sense [i.e., time] (B 158).

Kant footnoted his last use of the term existence in that quote, and, in the footnote, he echoes the problem from §16, this time saying that the solution to it would require a "self-intuiting." He then states that such self-intuition is "grounded" in the "form" of "time."

Thus, it is possible to characterize meaning-making regarding the existing individual because the meaning-making *acts* of the existing individual *necessarily* take place in time. Though this truth is clearly present in Kant's *Critique of Pure Reason* and is definitely a truth of transcendental philosophy, credit for popularizing the development of these Kantian insights goes, of course, to Heidegger's *Being & Time*.

Now, in the *Critique of Pure Reason* Kant does not develop the idea of the self-understanding of existence freely-making-meaning-in-regard-to-its-be-ing-in-time, yet, he provides a development of this idea elsewhere in his work *Religion within the Limits of Reason Alone* (1793).

Thus, on the one hand, for the purpose of articulating the archaeological answer to the question "What is existentialism?" we can refer to the result of Kant's development of this idea as "the three genera with which to thematize transcendental apperception." On the other hand, the genera relate to (though do not directly correspond to) the self-actualization principles of existentialism. And, as will be discussed below, the three genera may be understood – following Heidegger – as modes of mineness.

The three genera for Kant are "animality," "humanity," and "personality." Whereas Kant considered the first category to be devoid of reason, calling it "physical and purely mechanical," he considered the second category to be grounded in the ratio-nality of "comparison" (Kant, 1960: 34). Further, these three genera actually have a very deep history in Western philosophy. For example, as ethical categories, they can be found in both Plato and Aristotle (cf. Scalambrino, 2016).

Though it is tempting to read Kant's genera as referring to Empiricism and Rationalism with the third being Kant's Transcendental philosophy, that would be a mistake. Rather, from within transcendental philosophy they are associated with *subjective* sensibility, *objective* understanding and *transcendental* apperception, respectively, as contexts with which to make meaning of existence. Aristotle's characterizations of these genera are illuminating: pleasure, honor, and contemplation, respectively.

The "Philosophical Archaeology" Answer

To say that an existing individual contextualizes and thematizes their apperception with regard to these genera is to say that an existing individual determines and understands their be-ing-in-time with regard to these genera. In other words, it turns out these genera are the perennial-generic-philosophical contexts for determining and understanding the meaning of life. Specifically, then, as will be discussed in Volume II, Chapter 4, §8, these genera become the often mentioned "Modes of Mineness" in Heidegger's *Being & Time*. Indifference (§§14-34), Inauthenticity (§§35-38), and Authenticity (§§39-40 & §§45-60).

Interestingly, like all of the existentialists, Kant even states what he takes to be the motor force for moving toward the highest genus/context with which to determine and understand the meaning of existence. For Kant it is "respect" for the *necessity* involved in the transcendental dimension (cf. Kant, 1960; cf. Kant, 2017; cf. Wood, 2007).

Notice, Kant's idea here functions doubly in regard to existentialism. First, it may be understood as an articulation of be-ing-toward-death in Kant's philosophy; because the existing individual is ultimately mortal, its be-ing-in-time as an existing individual is finite; it *necessarily* must die. Second, it may be understood as indicating the path to self-actualization in that it offers us access to the truth of reality in the face of worldliness. Thus, respect for the necessary in Kant becomes anxiety in Kierkegaard, love of fate in Nietzsche, *Angst* in Heidegger, and dread in Sartre.

To conclude, this chapter provided *the archaeological answer to the question, "What is existentialism?"* The archaeological answer has priority over all the other answers to the question, especially because it provides the "Seven Principles of Existentialism," as these are the principles from which the topics and themes of existentialism stem.

The seven (7) principles are:

{*The Constitutional Principles*}
1) Mystery, or Existence Exceeds Consciousness;
2) Freedom, or Meaning-Making (Freedom to Determine & Understand One's Own Life);
3) Mineness, or the Mineness of Existence over Worldliness;
4) Anxiety, or Conscience and Care (this is the inverse of the *scala amoris* from Plato);

{*The Actualization Principles*}
5) Authenticity, or Be-ing-in-the-World;
6) Integrity, or the Resolute Be-ing-in-Time of Commitment;
7) Sincerity, or Be-ing-toward-Death.

In regard to the constitutional principles, (1) existence exceeds consciousness, that is, the order of existence is more primordial than the order of consciousness; (2) Kant considered spontaneity as evidence of transcendental freedom, and, thereby, we may say that the making of meaning in regard to existence manifests through action by a transcendentally-free individual. Thus, the principle of freedom indicates the transcendental freedom of the existing individual and the individual's freedom for self-realization and self-actualization; (3) the mineness of existence, that is, mineness over worldliness, ultimately refers to person-al, individual, transcendental be-ing; (4) anxiety from be-ing-in-the-world is also existentially constitutional. To exist is to be-in-the-world, and to be in the world is to experience Angst, anxiety.

The "Philosophical Archaeology" Answer

Anxiety is placed last on the list of constitutional principles as it also functions as the primary constitutional motor force potentiating self-actualization. Thus, it accounts for the motor force of how an existing individual changes the contexts with which it understands the meaning of its existence in terms of its relation to what is necessary in existence.

In regard to the principles of self-actualization, then, (5) "authenticity" refers to the most primordial determination possible of existence in terms of an individual's be-ing in time, and this is a mode of mineness revealed by living through resolution and commitment; (6) the self-understanding of the transcendental be-ing that is the existing individual determines its meaning in one of three contexts; just as meaning-making in terms of the transcendental context is the condition for the possibility of (re)integrating our dis-integrating be-ing-in-the-world, "integrity" refers to the resoluteness/commitment that allows for the actualization of be-ing-in-time-as-a-whole; lastly, (7) as a kind of focal point in regard to the other principles, "sincerity," as respect for the finitude/impermanence of existing, is the condition for owning one's death; it actualizes the be-ing-toward-the-end of oneself seen as a totality.

As noted above, whereas principles 1-3 & 6 all come from Kant's *Critique of Pure Reason*, principle 4 comes from his *Critique of Practical Reason*, his *The Metaphysics of Morals*, and his *Religion Within the Limits of Reason Alone*. Principles 6 & 7 can be found in both Kant's *Critique of Pure Reason* and his *Religion Within the Limits of Reason Alone*. These principles are discussed more thoroughly in the following chapters.

History of Philosophy Part I: Chapter 2. The "Historical Emergence of Existentialism as a Philosophical Theme" Answer: Existentialism as the Phoenix of Romanticism

> "We are close to waking
> When we dream that we are dreaming."
> ~Novalis,
> "Miscellaneous Observations,"
> *Philosophical Writings*, §16.

§0 Overview of Chapter 2

The purpose of this chapter – Chapter 2 – is to provide the first part of the "philosophical genealogy" answer to the question "What is existentialism?" Whereas the archaeological answer provided the principles for existential philosophy, Kant had not thematized the principles. The thematization began with German Romanticism prompted by way of the critique of Hegelian Idealism.

Thus, Chapter 2 Section 1 illustrates how German Romanticism understood the principle of mystery in terms of existence as Nature's creative power and the mineness of existence as Nature's work of art. The title of Section 2 references Julius von Leypold's (1804-1874) painting *Wanderer in the Storm* and Friedrich Nietzsche's (1844-1900) essay the "Wanderer and Its Shadow." We could just as easily also mention Caspar David Friedrich's (1774-1840) painting *Wanderer above the Sea of Fog*.

Sections 3 and 4 of Chapter 2, taken together, articulate the Romantic idea that can be understood in terms of apotheosis, philosophical alchemy, or self-actualization. This is because these principles can be thematized in a Romantic way: for example, they may be understood in terms of one overcoming the physical and social anchors holding one back from understanding the reality of one's true existence, that is, from remaining awake to the existence of the transcendental be-ing that one is.

Thus, Section 3 discusses the process through which the principles of Freedom, Anxiety, and Authenticity raise an individual's consciousness – raise an individual's awareness – to the point of a transcendental view of existence. Section 4, then, discusses the culmination of the process and the retrospective transcendental view of the process. In this way, the apotheosis itself may be seen as a joyful quest, that is, a quest to express the joy of transcendental be-ing.

Just as Kant pointed to respect for the necessary in existence as the motor force for what Romantically is understood as apotheosis, so too *Amor Fati* represents the love of the necessary in existence, allowing for it to be experienced as beauty and joy. In this way, Section 4 provides the Romantic articulation of integrity, authenticity, and sincerity – the transcendental be-ing-toward-our-own-death which allows us to live in the revelation of the truth of our existence.

§1 Existence as a Naturally-Creative Power: Meaning-Making and Life as a Work of Art

Given what was said in Chapter 1 regarding the relation between consciousness and existence, though the transcendental point of view brings the reality of existence into focus, it also brings into focus the limits of consciousness to understand existence. In other words, we are alienated from our own existence; this is a central tenet of Romanticism. We might paraphrase: My consciousness is always already consciousness of my alienation from reality. This is how it is possible to be "inauthentic." This is how it is possible to have one's consciousness "colonized."

Before this insight emerged as a central tenet of existential philosophy, the Romantics tended to express it – not in terms of existence, but – in terms of Nature. Thus, each individual (human) is an expression of the universal Spirit, and, because Spirit is alienated from Nature (a Mystery School theme preserved in Western philosophy through Plato), each individual consciousness is alienated from (its own) Nature.

To express this Romantically, we could say that the very consciousness with which we gain an understanding of the reality of Nature is the consciousness that obscures our ability to experience Nature as a paradise. If we wanted to state this more theologically, then, we could say: consciousness mediates our relation to divinity. By making our relation to Nature less immediate, it falls to the capacities of individuated consciousness to relate to the divinity within Nature and to Spirit as divine.

In this way, just as our relation to divinity in Nature is mediated – we can only view paradise through a glass darkly, as it were – so too our relation to the divinity of Spirit is mediated. Notice, on the one hand, that we require the transcendental point of view to apperceptively gain this awareness, and, on the other hand, notice how these insights themselves follow from developing the transcendental point of view with transcendental logic. In other words, the structure of the development of the insight gained in Chapter 1, §1 which led us to distinguish between transcendental psychology, cosmology, and theology, is the same (transcendental) logic that allowed us to articulate the above Romantic alienation from Nature.

Now, consider how the Romantics thought of consciousness. From the non-transcendental-points-of-view which had dominated modern philosophy until the time of Kant's Copernican Revolution, that is, the subjective and objective points of view can now be seen as "fallen" points of view. For, it is as if one has fallen into the *world*views of Subjectivity and Objectivity when one no longer has the transcendental world-view.[5]

Recall how consciousness is understood – from the transcendental point of view – as emerging from existence. That is to say, consciousness is ontologically-secondary to existence. In this way, the Romantics were able to honor poetic experience and, if we must use the term: poetic consciousness.

That is to say, when we ascend to the transcendental point of view, we bring our contact with reality into focus, and the process of making meaning from existence emerges through the quality of our contact with reality. Thus, because meaning emerges, that is, manifests, within consciousness, the process may be understood as "poetic" in a number of ways.

The term "poetic" comes from the ancient Greek *poeisis*, which means "to make" or to "bring into existence." Thus, from moment to moment what is made to exist – that which is different in each moment – may be understood as the poetic

---

[5] "Worldview" is actually a problematic term. It comes from the German *Weltanschauung*, which is better understood as referring to "a style of intuiting," that is, a "style of intuiting a world."

creation of Nature. As Schelling famously taught, since Nature is visible Spirit and Spirit is invisible Nature, the poetic creation of the here and now is natural, spiritual, and divine. The existence of each individual participates in that divine process, as a poet, making meaning of existing. In this way, life itself is a work of art, we are all artists, and we are all works of art.

It may be helpful to juxtapose two quotes here, one from Novalis and one from Nietzsche. Notice Novalis' word choice in his teaching: "Only an artist can divine the meaning of life."[6] And, here we hear an echo in a teaching from Nietzsche:

> In song and in dance man expresses himself as a member of a higher community... He is no longer an artist; he has become a work of art... to the sound of the chisel strokes of the Dionysian world-artist rings out the cry of the Eleusinian mysteries ... 'Do you sense your Maker, world?'[7]

Of course, the ontology and the logic in which these quotes participate are completely transcendental. There is a cosmos, you are a part of the cosmos, and the vision to which we can ascend and the meaning out of it we are able *to make* is relative to our ability to re-turn to Spirit – to lessen our alienation from Spirit. Because Spirit is divine, Novalis was correct to suggest that this process of lessening our alienation from Nature by ascending to the transcendental point of view is actually an apotheosis.[8]

---

[6] "Logological Fragments I," §96.
[7] *The Birth of Tragedy*, §1.
[8] Though this may already be understood as a "quest" to accomplish the apotheosis of ascending to the transcendental point of view in the

The meaning of existence depends on the quality of one's contact with reality, and that quality is determined by the extent of one's apotheosis, of one's self-actualization. To accomplish an ascension to the transcendental point of view is to determine and understand the poetic meaning-making of existence as an individuated expression of universal be-ing, that is, as the (art) work of Spirit through Nature as universal be-ing.

Here, then, is the ontological point of departure from which Romanticism could transform fully into both art and an existential philosophy. Though Novalis taught us well when he said that "The artist is completely transcendental"[9] and an existential philosopher may, of course, be an artist, the difference is that as existentialism emerges from Romanticism, it remains a transcendental *philosophy*. In this way, just as transcendental philosophy refers to a scientific approach to ontology, so too 20th century existentialism may be understood as a science of existence, a science of being in time.

§2 The *Wanderer in the Storm* & *The Wanderer and Its Shadow*

Perhaps the painting most often associated with (especially) 19th century) existentialism is Caspar David Friedrich's *Wanderer above the Sea of Fog* (c. 1818).[10] However, the painting the *Wanderer in the Storm* by Julius von Leypold (c. 1835) represents well what we have been discussing in this chapter. In fact, the following description of Leypold's painting from The Metropolitan Museum of Art may be helpful:

---

writings of Novalis, Nietzsche makes it explicit. Thus, *Die fröhliche Wissenschaft* as *The Joyful Quest*.
[9] "Logological Fragments I," §34.
[10] This is the painting on the cover of Volume II of this two-volume set.

> The figure of a wanderer in an untamed natural setting personified restless yearning [alienation] for the German Romantics...

Along these lines, Nietzsche's essay "The Wanderer and Its Shadow," found in the third part of *Human, All Too Human*, may be seen as a philosophical development of the Romantic theme.

In other words, it is as if for each individual existence – each individuated existence – consciousness may be understood as its Shadow. This is an especially Romantic characterization of consciousness as "fallen," "worldly," consciousness, and in this way Nietzsche's existential philosophy may be understood as a non-religious, philosophical, attempt to go beyond the yearning-alienation-centered *Weltanschauung* of German Romanticism.

To be operating with a lower genera/context for determining and understanding the meaning of existence is to be be-ing-in-the-world with a lower mode of mineness, and, recall, it is as if mineness and worldliness are on opposite ends of a spectrum. Therefore, to relate to universal (transcendental) be-ing with a lower context is to have fallen into worldliness. Of course, to have fallen into the world is to be alienated from one's *natural* (spiritual) be-ing. Thus, to ascend to the transcendental point of view is to envision the truth of one's becoming, despite alienated individuated be-ing-in-the-world.

The theme of this section, then, is the discussion of the genealogy of the philosophical development of German Romanticism into existentialism. The theme of re-turning to Spirit through suffering is portrayed by the theme of the "Storm," in Leypold's painting. And, the anonymity of the "Wanderer" poetically captures alienated, individuated, Spirit – the existential reality of being alienated from an authentic engagement with existence, alienated from an authentic engagement with the mineness of one's own existence.

As was noted just above regarding Novalis – and the theme is also explicit in Hölderlin and Schelling – we suffer from placing our faith in a fallen consciousness. We suffer from believing that fallen consciousness reveals the truth of existence. Of course, the Romantic theme of "suffering from the point of view of being an individuation of Nature" receives its crowning expression in Schopenhauer's philosophy. Yet, what is also common to all of these philosophers is the theme that through such suffering we may arrive at, ascend to, or accomplish the apotheosis of the transcendental point of view.

To rise above the fog of alienated individuated spirit's worldly consciousness is to actualize the transcendental point of view regarding the world.

§3 From the Mourning of the Future to the Dawning of Eternity: The Truth of Undying Love and Alienation as the Cost of the Freedom to Witness the Future of Your Spiritual Self

It is possible to provide a list of Romantic themes, which would also be a list of existential themes, especially: Death, Love, Freedom, and Alienation. Further, at the intersection of these themes, we would find themes such as Beauty and Despair, and gain access to questions regarding Divinity, Nihilism, Meaninglessness, Truth and Justice.

It is also possible to recognize a pivotal point in the historical emergence of existentialism regarding the theme of Death. It is helpful to recognize that the form of the conversation regarding Love was already set for philosophy by Plato. Specifically, Plato's famous *scala amoris* from his dialogues *Symposium* and *Phaedrus*. As *scala*, "ladder or stairway," suggests, love may characterize relations along the ascension to what we now – following Kant – can call the transcendental point of view.[11]

Though the following paraphrase is a reduction of the complexity found in Plato's *Symposium*, it is nonetheless helpful: Conscious awareness of love may be understood along the trajectory of the ascension to the transcendental point of view. That is to say, aesthetic consciousness loves bodies, herd consciousness loves social status, and the transcendental point of view brings the Spirit of Love into focus,[12] and allows for genuine communion in love.

Thus, when we fall in love with another person, from the transcendental point of view, it is clear that we will eventually lose contact with that person. We will eventually lose the ability to physically relate to their bodies, and we will eventually lose the harmony we experience in the relation between our hearts, that is, the affective cores of our beings, the *mind-external* relational parts of what we may call our souls.

Because of these eventual truths, the experience of love may be understood as already containing a tinge of the loss of love. This may be Romantically expressed in terms of mourning

---

[11] Interestingly, it is as if the transcendental point of view is both the condition for the possibility of an existential philosophy and the philosophical goal of existence, that is, arriving at the best point of view for "Knowing Yourself." Moreover, it should not be surprising that the understanding of falling and be-ing alienated (from transcendental be-ing) in the world would be the inverse of Plato's *scala amoris*, which characterizes the trajectory toward the transcendental point of view.

[12] The reason I constructed this sentence in such a general fashion was to allow for reference to the multiple styles with which philosophers have expressed existentialism. In other words, one could equally say: "God is Love," the "Reality of Love," or the "Love of Fate" into focus.

the loss of love and the future. In fact, a Romantic may claim, it is not possible to completely love someone without the awareness of the reality of love's temporary nature. Thus, in the future of this love we will mourn its loss, and just as this mourning of the future approaches nearer each moment, not knowing the moment of its arrival amounts to its being present now through its futural-absence.

The ability to change in the now for the sake of the future is known by everyone. This insight links with the themes of suffering and ascension – both in terms of the *scala amoris*, self-actualization, and apotheosis – as it helps bring into focus our contact with the *sublime necessity* of reality. How did we meet this person that we love? How were we in such a psychological state when we met them that we could "fall in love" with them? Think of all the stars that needed to align, all of the events which needed to occur, for us to even have the chance to fall in love. And, so on... This is perfectly expressed by Keats in his poem "When I have fears":

> "When I behold, upon the night's starr'd face,
> Huge cloudy symbols of a high romance,
> And think that I may never live to trace
> Their shadows, with the magic hand of chance;
> And when I feel, fair creature of an hour,
> That I shall never look upon thee more..."

If we look back from the transcendental point of view, envisioning the experience of love along the *scala amoris*, it is possible to envision the "fall" and the "ascension" as themselves necessary aspects of the reality of existence; for, if philosophers are correct, then these aspects may be understood as *necessary* parts of each individual's experience of reality; that is not to say that some specific experience will necessarily happen; rather, it is to say that, experience itself depends on these aspects.

Thus, the *scala amoris* may be understood, ontologically, as the potential for each individual to become aware of, and *participate* in, the highest and purest form of love. This form of love is the purest form of love because it does not die, despite the manner in which Nature changes. In this way, one, we might come to understand transcendental love as the acme of Spirit. It is a love that remains love. And, thus, two, it is also a glimpse into the eternal Nature of love.

This transcendental realization – this actualization of the capacity to love – has the power to re-contextualize the truth of consciousness' alienation from the reality of existence. In other words, alienation may be seen as the condition for the possibility of witnessing our transcendental freedom to relate to existence in multiple ways, for example, along the *scala*. When seen this way, it is as if alienation is the price we pay to find transcendental love (Heidegger called this "care").

What is more, this realization may be understood as indicating a philosophical point of transition from Romanticism to existentialism. Especially if we think of Romanticism and existentialism as two different constellations of – or ways of constellating – the ideas of transcendental philosophy, then, it is as if this realization indicates a shift from the primacy of alienation to the primacy of freedom. And, with the primacy of freedom, then, existentialism emerges from Romanticism.

§4 *Amor Fati*: The Joyful Quest

The Romantic idea of a *potential* for *apotheosis* – brought into transcendental philosophy by Novalis – was fashioned into an existential quest by Nietzsche. Recalling what was just said in section two of this chapter, above, about "the Wanderer," on the one hand, from some points of view along the trajectory of one's *apotheosis*, the value of certain forms of life simply can't be seen. Thus, expressing the truth of individuated (mind-external) existence with which we must always already cope and which we always already identify as ours, that is, with a form of "mineness," strikes some people as reductive, until they can see *that* (Wanderer, e.g., the Fool in the Tarot) as the true ground of their existence. In other words, the *apotheosis* is always already transcendentally perspectival.[13]

On the other hand, when one recognizes the primacy of existence in regard to *the experience of* this life, then it becomes possible to understand it as *the* real source of mystery. Even if divinity has no physical aspect toward which we can relate, it is through the experience of reality that one comes to, or arrives at, their understanding of and relation to divinity. In other words, the structure of an *apotheosis* – spanning a spectrum from individual existence to the point of view one develops out of it and uses to interpret it – can be interpreted as progressing toward, at least, a focal point.

Of course, that focal point – as noted above – is the transcendental point of view. Thus, Nietzsche's moves are actually quite intuitive in that he constellated the very ideas inherited from German Romanticism. Further, if through the experience of this life one can bring their contact with the sublime reality of transcendental necessity into focus, then it is possible to relate to *that* aspect of existence. Though,

---

[13] The ontology of self-actualization is perspectival in terms of the self and world projected by the different stages along its development. And, its perspectival character allows us to characterize it in terms of the structure of experience culminating in transcendental apperception.

The "Historical Emergence ... as a Philosophical Theme" Answer

structurally speaking, that contact belongs to the context of transcendental theology, it can be characterized atheistically.

Thus, *existentialism does not force an interpretation of the meaning to be made from one's experience of life, rather, it seeks to uncover the conditions for the possibility of the meaning made from one's experience of life.* Insofar as these conditions are universal – and, according to Kant, they, of course, are universal to the species – it becomes possible to articulate them *both* perspectivally and scientifically.

In fact, we could go so far as to say that 19th century existentialism emphasized the former and 20th century existentialism emphasized the latter. That is why 20th century existentialism became popularly understood as atheistic, because the "scientific" interpretation of its philosophical structure became historically and culturally dominant.

Yet, we should emphasize two points here: First, those interpretations are neither incommensurable with one another nor is either one of them simply the sublation of the other. In other words, picking one interpretation doesn't make the truth of the other impossible, and even though we can situate one of the interpretations as falling within the interpretive framework of the other, the philosophical structure of the difference between the two is ultimately undecidable.

This is why, the "true" existentialist takes issue with being called an "existentialist," especially insofar as that is supposed to preemptively mean some interpretation or another of what the transcendental point of view brings into focus. Second, it is possible to continuously toggle between these interpretations toward illuminating the historical emergence of existentialism as a philosophical theme – out of transcendental philosophy – through Romanticism.

Finally, then, in this way, notice that Nietzsche's *Amor Fati* is the love of the *necessary in existence*. That which is technically – within transcendental philosophy – the indicator of transcendental theology, and, thus, divinity. Hence, Nietzsche's *Amor Fati* represents the transition of Romantic apotheosis to existential self-actualization.

For an extensive discussion of *Amor Fati* see my *Full Throttle Heart: The Rapture & Ecstasy of Nietzsche's Dionysian Worldview*. For our purpose, the following discussion of *Amor Fati* by way of juxtaposing a number of Nietzsche quotes – especially from *Die fröhliche Wissenschaft*, aka *The Cheerful Science* or *The Joyful Quest* – should be sufficient.

From *Beyond Good & Evil* §17, I would like to highlight Nietzsche's use of four, intimately-related, terms: "superstition," "supposition," "interpretation," and "process."

> With regard to the superstitions of logicians, I shall never tire of emphasizing a small terse fact, which these superstitious minds hate to concede – namely, that a thought comes when "it" wishes, and not when "I" wish, so that it is a falsification of the facts of the case to say that the subject "I" is the condition for the predicate "think." *It* thinks; but that this "it" is precisely the famous old "ego" is, to put it mildly, only a supposition, an assertion, and assuredly not an "immediate certainty." After all, one has even gone too far with this "it thinks" – even the "it" contains an *interpretation* of the process, and does not belong to the process itself.

Notice that, there is the process itself, there are interpretations of the process, there are the various pathways into the interpretations of the process, and there is the transcendental point of view bringing it all into focus.

In light of this, consider the following from *The Joyful Quest*, Book 5, §346.

> The whole pose of "man *against* the world," of man as a "world-negating" principle, of man as the measure of the value of things, as judge of the world who in the end places *existence* [emphasis added] itself upon his scales and finds it wanting – the monstrous insipidity of this pose has finally come home to us and we are sick of it... And, thus, also pessimism, the contempt for that existence which is knowable by *us*? Have we not exposed ourselves to the suspicion of an opposition – an opposition between the world in which we were at home up to now with our reverences that perhaps made it possible for us to endure life, and another world that consists of us – an inexorable, fundamental, and deepest suspicion about ourselves that is more and more gaining worse and worse control of us... and that could easily confront coming generations with the terrifying Either/Or: "Either abolish your reverences or- *yourselves*!" The latter would be nihilism; but would not the former also be – nihilism? – This is *our* question mark.

Especially in regard to Nietzsche's emphasis of the "Either/Or" way of characterizing possibility, we can see that "the process" of existence is *beyond either/or*.

Later, also in Book 5 of *The Joyful Quest*, though this time §354, the transcendental philosophizing of Nietzsche can also be seen as he articulates his understanding of the relation between consciousness and existence.

> It was only as a social animal that man acquired self-consciousness – which he is still in the process of doing, more and more.
>
> My idea is, as you see, that *consciousness does not really belong to man's individual existence* [emphasis added] but rather to his social or herd nature; that, as follows from this, it has developed subtlety only insofar as this is required by social or herd utility.

Thus, Nietzsche transcendentally locates consciousness – the making conscious of the *process of existence* – as an existential power in the service of communal dwelling, that is, domestication. Moreover, not only is consciousness the condition for the possibility of self-consciousness; but also, the interpretative nature of consciousness is even more noticeable when it comes to self-consciousness.

It is not just that we have been trained to interpret existence in ways beneficial to the goals and values of those who trained us; rather, the very categories on which their trainings depend are suppositions and superstitions. Yet, despite the constitutionally-interpretative nature of consciousness and the insight into transcendental undecidability here, existence continues to exist, the process remains more primordial than all insights which emerge from it.

Having said all that, we are ready to read the *Amor Fati* passage from Book 4, §276 of *The Joyful Quest*:

> *To the new year* – Still I live, still I think: I must still live, then I must still think... Today everyone allows the speaking out of wishful and

> heartfelt thinking: so now I also want to say, what I wish for myself today and which thought first ran across my heart this year, – which thought shall be my foundation, certainty, and sweetness for the rest of my life! I want to learn more and more, to see the necessary in things as beautiful: – then I will be one who makes things beautiful. *Amor Fati*: shall be my love from now on! I do not want to wage war on what is ugly. I do not want to accuse, I do not even want to accuse the accusers. Looking away will be my only negation. And, all in all and on the whole: I wish to be only a Yes-sayer! (Nietzsche, 1974: 223). [14]

Notice, the beginning of the passage coincides with an existential critique of Descartes (I think, therefore I am). Further, in regard to the end of the passage, this kind of "transcendental" Yes-saying relates to existence, it relates to the necessary (fated) aspects of existence. Interestingly, though this relation is to fate, not destiny, it also has consequences for destiny.[15]

On the one hand, consider the last epigram prior to *Amor Fati*: "What is the seal of liberation? – No longer being ashamed in front of oneself." This can be understood as describing the individual's destiny to "become who they are."

---

[14] This comes from my *Full Throttle Heart*: "Because this book represents the kind of "conquest" of love described in the songs of the "Knight-Poets" – "that unity of singer, knight, and free spirit." (cf. *Ecce Homo*). In this way, *Amor Fati* represents a kind of culmination and ecstatic moment in the Knight-Poet's quest for joyousness."

[15] Fate is necessary; destiny is potential.

(Book III, §275). The difference between: (the incongruence stemming from the difference between an individual's view of itself, from itself) and (the individual's view of itself, as it *supposes* it is seen from the point of view of culture and society). This incongruence is a kind of "bad faith" in one's self that functions as a catalyst for "inauthenticity." Thus, to fulfill the destiny to become who one is, is to ascend to the *Amor Fati*, and – in breaking this seal – conquer the prize of the joyful quest.

On the other hand, recall Nietzsche's comments from *Ecce Homo: How One Becomes What One Is* (1888), especially, the chapter "Why I Am So Clever," §10.

> My formula for greatness is *amor fati*: that you do not want anything to be different, not forwards, not backwards, not for all eternity. Not just to tolerate *necessity* [emphasis added], still less to conceal it ... but to *love* it...

All of the major Romantic elements we have been discussing in this chapter can now be seen. The necessary (constitutional) aspects of the "Wanderer's" existence, that is, (i) existence individuated, (ii) consciousness as always already alienated from existence, (iii) a perspectival trajectory of apotheosis and (iv) a quest to traverse the non-transcendentally-constituted, "lower," perspectives toward the attainment of the perspective that is its own reward.

There is existence, there is meaning-making, and there is potential for the development of a relation to the necessity *of* existence and the necessary *in* existence – these "pieces of fate" – that constitute and clarify the very individuation of *existence*. This "formula for greatness," this quest, this *apotheosis* is a transcendental characterization of *the process of existence*.

History of Philosophy Part II: Chapter 3. The "Philosophical Genealogy" Answer: From Germany to France: Schelling, Schopenhauer, Kierkegaard, Nietzsche, Heidegger, Sartre, and Marcel

> "Just as Spirit is invisible Nature, Nature should be Spirit made visible. Here then, in the absolute identity of Spirit in us and Nature outside us, the problem of the possibility of a Nature external to us must be resolved."
> ~F.W.J. Schelling,
> *Ideas for a Philosophy of Nature*. (1989: 42).

§0 Overview of Chapter 3

The purpose of this chapter – Chapter 3 – is to provide the second part of the "philosophical genealogy" answer to the question "What is existentialism?" This second part looks more like what one might usually expect from a genealogy. Thus, the sections of Chapter 3 each provide a characterization of a major existentialist philosopher in regard to how they express the seven principles of existentialism and how they instantiate the existentialist framework (Chapter 1, above), in terms of their ontologies and in terms of their ethics.

Thus, the following sections present the major *philosophers* of the history of existentialism in terms of the constitutional principles (mystery, freedom, mineness, and anxiety) and the actualization principles (authenticity, integrity, and sincerity) of existentialism. A similar juxtaposition appears in Vol. II, Ch. 5, §10, "The Moment of Vision."

§1 Existentialism against Hegel's Resurrection of Enlightenment Rationalist Nihilisms: the Nihilism of Being-as-History and the Nihilism of Being-as-Speculative-System

The following two paragraphs come from my chapter: "Being in the Continental Tradition: Phenomenological Hermeneutics as Fundamental Ontology." (Scalambrino, 2020b: 83).

The initial reception of Immanuel Kant's (1724-1804) transcendental philosophy was thoroughly polemical and negative. As a kind of response, Karl Leonhard Reinhold constructed a series of articles in letter form – hence, the *Letters on the Kantian Philosophy* – between August, 1786 and September, 1787. Because these letters functioned as the catalyst for [a kind of] Homeric Contest, it is worth asking: What was Reinhold's motivation for writing them?

In multiple ways, Reinhold's letters may be read as prompted by the publication of a set of letters directed, not at Kant's philosophy but, at the philosophy of Baruch/Benedict Spinoza (1632-1677). These letters, published in 1785, written between Friedrich Heinrich Jacobi (1743-1819) and Moses Mendelssohn (1729-1786), popularized the idea that the Rationalist philosophy of the "Age of Reason," or the "Enlightenment," ultimately leads to "nihilism." On the one hand, Jacobi took Spinoza's philosophy to be the most systematically-coherent of the all the Rationalist philosophers. On the other hand, just as Spinoza's philosophy was understood to culminate in "pantheism" and, thereby, "atheism" – because it is the most representative of the Rationalist-Enlightenment project – Jacobi concluded that *all* rationalistic philosophy is ultimately atheistic and *nihilistic*.

The "Philosophical Genealogy" Answer

This is the proper historical understanding of why Hegel's critics invoked the charge of "nihilism" against him, that is, Hegel took Kant's insights and attempted to revert them into a "rationalistic" context. Now, the existentialist critique of G.W.F. Hegel (1770-1831) is one of those topics that could seemingly be discussed to no end. However, we should be able to point directly to the heart of the dispute, if we follow Kierkegaard's lead by focusing on the two aspects of Hegel's philosophy which prompted his formulation of an "existential philosophy" to combat it.

It is important to be clear here regarding the way we are approaching and interpreting Hegel's philosophy, because existentialists have leaned toward Hegel in different ways; what I mean by this is that there are clearly Hegelian figurations and phrases running through Heidegger and Sartre, and though those Hegelian elements may be philosophically problematic in regard to the way an existentialist articulates their ontology, *those elements* are, ultimately, insufficient to negate the philosophies as "existential."

Of course, it was Kierkegaard's critique of Hegel's philosophy in favor of Kant that is often cited as the beginning of the history of existentialism. However, when we focus directly on the aspects of Hegel's philosophy critiqued by Kierkegaard, then we gain three insights.

First, these same elements of Hegel's philosophy were criticized by F.W.J. Schelling (1775-1854) and Arthur Schopenhauer (1788-1860), prior to Kierkegaard's criticisms. In this way, Kierkegaard – who attended Schelling's Berlin lectures critiquing Hegel – can be seen as participating in a tradition that stems directly from Kant. Second, the first insight also helps us recognize that it was Hegel's philosophy that deviated Kant's revolutionary philosophy back toward Cartesianisms that are, ultimately, incommensurable with the spirit of Kant's philosophy. In other words, the second insight here is that existentialism directly stems from (a proper reading of) Kant's transcendental philosophy. Lastly, the specific criticisms on which this chapter focuses are present among all the existentialists – even the ones by whom other Hegelian elements are embraced.

Combining everything that has been stated so far in this section, then, we can recognize why the existentialists (especially Kierkegaard and Nietzsche) thought of Hegel's rationalistically-systematic philosophy as nihilistic. Specifically, existentialists attack Hegel's philosophy in two places. It is helpful to refer to those places as: "the Nihilism of Being-as-History" and "the Nihilism of Being-as-Speculative-System."

As can be seen by way of both the archaeological and the genealogical answers to the question "What is existentialism?" the actualization principles combat "the Nihilism of Being-as-History" and the constitutional principles combat "the Nihilism of Being-as-Speculative-System." To clarify this further, consider the following brief discussion of death.

From the point of view of the existing individual, death immediately illuminates "the Nihilism of Being-as-History" by showing us that the meaning of our be-ing-in-time is not simply the general characterizations of everydayness constituted, for example, by whatever is "trending." In other words, the everyday narrative that reckons history as a "definite picture" is inauthentic and nihilistic. Heidegger understood this in terms of the difference between authentic History (*Geschichte*) and inauthentic History as *Historie*.

The "Philosophical Genealogy" Answer

By way of Heidegger's *Contributions to Philosophy* (1936-1938) the following paraphrase from Michael Inwood's *A Heidegger Dictionary* expresses the existentialist critique well: "*Historie* causally explains the past and 'objectifies' it, in terms of the present, not the future. It serves man's will to establish himself in a 'surveyable order,' and degenerates into journalism." (Inwood, 1999: 92). Going even further:

> *Historie* thinks causally, making life and experience accessible to causal calculation, and unable to recognize that historical beings have a different mode of being. It regiments its object for exploitation and 'breeding'... *Historie* involves comparison, and its 'progress' consists in the replacement of one respect of comparison by another; the respect adopted reflects the present in which the historian stands. The 'discovery of so-called new "material" is always the consequence, not the ground, of the newly selected respect of explanation' and comparison... In the hands of *Historie* history becomes ahistorical: 'Blood and race become the bearers of history.' (Inwood, 1999: 92).

In terms of the philosophical (archaeological) framework of existentialism, notice the repetition of the word "comparison" throughout the above quote. Just as this signals *Historie* and "the Nihilism of Being-as-History" grounded in what Kant called the predisposition of humanity, so too it is (be-ing-toward) death that actualizes us out of that inauthentic mode of be-ing.

It is the concern for one's death that makes your time existing more *meaningful* than the journalist's generality. Put another way, death raises us out of the lower (humanity) context for determining and understanding the *meaning* of life and places us in the personal dimension. Death may be seen converging existentially, here, with freedom, regarding "the Nihilism of Being-as-Speculative-System" in that, as Kierkegaard put it, "the abstract doesn't exist."

In other words, the speculative consideration of life *in general*, even if objective, is less efficacious than commitment. We are free, and be-ing free, we must choose our actions. And, as Sartre liked to emphasize, freedom – just like death – is inescapable. Choosing not to choose is still making a choice. Though existentialists strive to bring the reality of existence into focus, we see narratives (ontologically) as grounded in the freedom of existence. That is to say, for existentialism, people are more primordial than any systematic narrative that seemingly puts them in a neat little box.

Thus, relating to death clears an authentic space for integrity and sincerity by way of commitment to the future. In fact, for existentialists, because relating to the future is necessarily an ontological aspect of existence, conscience and anxiety naturally arise when we apperceive in terms of the lower contexts for determining and understanding the meaning of life.[16] The existing individual is always already more than the narrative or speculative system that "explains" them, because the narrative always already depends on how the existing individual chooses to live their life (the finite amount of time they have to exist).

---

[16] Heidegger even went so far as to call this feeling arising out of the necessity of the ontological structure of existing "guilt." Interestingly, just as impatience is its own punishment, so too is nihilism. Making meaning of the world in terms of the lower contexts (animality and humanity) necessarily brings forth anxiety and the call of conscience.

In other words, relating to death clears a space for what Heidegger famously termed "one's ownmost potential," which existentialists contrast with the power of narrative. Narrative can lie in a way that existence can't. When you consider what it is that you *can do*, that is, what it is that you have the potential, the (will-to-) power, to do, then you are considering your ownmost potential. Of course, this involves taking into consideration the opportunities presently available to you, some of which are out of your control. Yet, the existentialist point here is that we cannot truly see our ownmost potential unless we develop the point of view that brings our (finite) be-ing-in-time to our awareness.

To conclude this section, then, notice that – genealogically speaking – existentialism returns to the spirit of Kant's transcendental philosophy by critiquing two nihilisms brought (back) into the history of Western philosophy by Hegel, namely, "the Nihilism of Being-as-History" and "the Nihilism of Being-as-Speculative-System." Just as these Hegelianisms result from a return to the (overly) rationalistic philosophy originated by Descartes, so too existential philosophers find themselves combating the equally nihilistic "Cartesian Legacy" still prevalent in the history of Western philosophy.

§2 Schelling's Positive Philosophy & Schopenhauer's Philosophy of Life

It is important to mention F.W.J. Schelling's (1775-1854) positive philosophy and Arthur Schopenhauer's (1788-1860) philosophy of life, so that we can see the trajectory of existential philosophy from Kant. Otherwise, we may fail to recognize that protests to the philosophies of Descartes and Hegel were already happening, prior to Kierkegaard's critiques.

This section is divided into the following sub-sections: {1} positive (existential) philosophy versus negative (rationalistic) philosophy; {2} from Nature to existence in light of fate; {3} the world is a re-presentation of present Nature; {4} Schelling's philosophy of nature and Schopenhauer's philosophy of life contain all the principles of existentialism.

{1} Schelling's critique of Hegel's philosophy appears in its perhaps most potent form at the end of his career. Schelling moved to Berlin in 1841 to occupy the academic position that was previously Hegel's until his death in 1831. Schelling's Berlin lectures have come to be published as *The Grounding of Positive Philosophy* (2012). I appreciate the blurb placed on the back cover of the English translation by SUNY Press:

> The Berlin lectures in *The Grounding of Positive Philosophy* ... advance Schelling's final "existential system" as an alternative to modernity's reduction of philosophy to a purely formal science of reason. The onetime protégé of Fichte and benefactor of Hegel, Schelling accuses German Idealism of dealing "with the world of lived experience just as a surgeon who promises to cure your ailing leg by amputating it." Schelling's appeal in Berlin for a positive, existential philosophy found an ... audience in Kierkegaard, Engels, Feuerbach, Marx...

What the back cover doesn't mention is Schelling's existential philosophy was a development of his philosophy of nature.

The idea here is that both Schelling and Schopenhauer discussed mind-external reality as "Nature." Thus, it is in terms of nature that they critique the nihilistic over-rationalizing of Hegel. However, keeping Kant's philosophy in mind as the

The "Philosophical Genealogy" Answer

framework within which they were working, "Nature" for Schelling and Schopenhauer referred precisely to what the later existential philosophers would call "existence."

Thus, Schelling's promotion of a "positive" philosophy is the promotion of an existential philosophy over a "negative" (nihilistic) rational philosophy. According to Schelling,

> That a plant in general exists is nothing contingent if anything in general exists: it is not contingent that there are plants in general, but there are no plants that exist in general, since there exists only this determinate plant at this point in space and in this moment of time. If I then also realize ... that in the cycle of existence in general plants must occur, with this insight I have still not moved beyond the concept of the plant. This plant is still not the real plant, but rather just the concept of the plant. (2012: 130).

For Schelling, the positive philosophy does not deal in generalities, it concerns itself with the *existing* particulars.

Schelling provided the following subsequent restatement and clarification of his position in terms of space and time:

> Conversely, reality does nothing to the whatness and the [logical] necessity that is independent of all reality. Thus, for example, the indivisibility of space is not a matter of real space, and what is in real space – order, symmetry, and definition – is all of a logical origin. In this way one may comprehend the importance of that distinction. Reason provides the content for everything that occurs in

> experience; it comprehends what is *real*, but not, therefore, *reality*. This is an important difference. (Schelling, 2012: 130).

With this clarification comes an insight at the heart of both Kierkegaard and Nietzsche, namely, logical necessity can blind us from our potential. A motivational poster would say some version of: "You are more than you *think* you are." In other words, existence is more than the "either/or" of logical necessity. And, it is important to always remember that the logic of either/or is driven by the principle of non-contradiction (PNC), and the PNC is also known as the "principle of unrestricted *generality*."

Later in the same work, Schelling clarifies his position again with explicit reference to Kant and Hegel.

> If we want anything that exists outside of thought, then we *must* proceed from a being that is absolutely independent of all thought, which precedes all thought. Of this being, the Hegelian philosophy knows nothing, it has no place for this concept. Kant has in mind that which necessarily exists…" (2012: 161).

It is worth noting that Schelling refers to mind-external reality here as be-ing and existence. Thus, this quote showcases both Hegel's philosophy as the overly-rationalistic negative philosophy *par excellence*, and provides one of Schelling's many acknowledgements of his debt to Kant's guidance.

Further, in these same lectures, he specifically associates positive philosophy with Kant's practical philosophy, which is, of course, from where we obtained the remainder of the principles of existentialism after mining Kant's *Critique of Pure Reason* for the initial principles manifest through his

Copernican Revolution. Moreover, Schelling consistently applied Kant's framework while striving to push transcendental philosophy forward. In his *On the History of Modern Philosophy*, Schelling explained, "Real thinking is where something which is opposed to thinking is overcome." (1994: 145). Of course, as developed by the existentialist's there is a certain logical or rational momentum that can spiritually drag us down, for example, Nietzsche called it "slave mentality," and it must be overcome, if we are to find our ownmost potential.

In fact, what was essentially canonized for existentialism in Heidegger's language from *Being & Time*, the concepts of potential and the future and their interrelatedness were actually already articulated by Schelling.

Again, through an accurate use of Kant's terminology, Schelling refers to the transcendental be-ing that is the ground of the existing individual as "the abyss."[17] He also calls it the *Ur-Grund* and *Unvordenklichkeit* (un-pre-think-able). Thus, the future comes from the abyss, from the ground. In fact, there is nowhere else from which it could come. This is why we ultimately think of chronological time (and *Historie*) as a construct. The idea of chronological time, especially – the idea, and grammar, of time as linear *progress* – projects a future as if it were *ex nihilo*, that is, coming from nothing. Yet, according to Schelling's *Romantische Naturphilosophie*, the future comes from the un-pre-think-able ground. And, that primal ground – still turbid in its depths – is, precisely, eternally-cycling Nature. (cf. Schelling, 2019).

{2} As one last example, from Schelling's early writings, we can already see his concern to think into that dimension of

---

[17] Compare this, for further elucidation, to the epigraph of this chapter.

transcendental freedom and fate, beyond what the mortal mind can fully comprehend:

> Many times, the question has been asked how Greek reason could bear the contradictions of Greek tragedy. A mortal, destined by fate to become a malefactor and himself fighting *against* this fate, is nevertheless appallingly punished for the crime, although it was the deed of destiny! The ground of this contradiction... lay in the contest between human freedom and the power of the objective world in which the mortal must succumb *necessarily* if that power is absolutely superior, if it is fate... That the malefactor who succumbs under the power of fate was punished, this tragic fact was the recognition of human freedom; it was the *honor* due to freedom. Greek tragedy honored human freedom, letting its hero *fight* against the superior power of fate. (Schelling, 1980: 192-3).

So much could be unpacked and discussed from this gorgeous passage. However, given the purpose of this section, let us at least note the following. The words "contradiction," "freedom," and "objective"/objectivity all appear in this passage. The focus is transcendental, that is, on the necessary in existence. Moreover, Schelling indicates how a mortal existence can be lived with a kind of nobility, that is, authenticity, integrity, and sincerity, despite being "condemned by fate."[18]

---

[18] Thus, to consider Jean-Paul Sartre or Viktor Frankl the origin of this kind of thinking is a mistake. Not only is it infused in the very ink with which Nietzsche wrote, but it is also – as presented by Schelling – exemplary of the culture of the ancient Greeks.

The "Philosophical Genealogy" Answer

{3} Arthur Schopenhauer was notorious for his critiques of Hegel and Hegel's philosophy. Nietzsche's calling Schopenhauer's philosophy a "pessimistic Romanticism" would not make sense if Schopenhauer did not conceive of nature and fate as a mind-external reality against which the existing individual struggles. This insight finds expression even regarding seemingly practical matters considered by Schopenhauer's thought. For example, from his *On Philosophy at the Universities*, "The vocation of philosophy can only be given by nature, not by the popular vote of bureaucratic administrators at a university." (2020: §31).

Similarly, Schopenhauer provided the history of existentialism with a Kantian emphasis seen in the very title of what is considered his greatest work, the two-volume set: *The World as Will & Representation*. That is to say, "the world" in which you dwell is "your representation" and, in some intimate way, associated with your will. This phenomenological insight, ultimately, from Kant can be heard in Heidegger's discussion of how we determine the meaning of and understand our future, and Sartre's discussion of the sense in which we are radically responsible for our choices and the world they create.

At the same time, Schopenhauer also highlights the sense for existentialism of (a) how mineness is to be emphasized over worldliness and (b) how an existing individual's authentic temporality is to be associated with transcendental be-ing.

> The more clearly you become conscious of the frailty, vanity, and dream-like quality of all things, *the more clearly will you also become conscious of the eternity of your own inner being*; because it is only in contrast to this that the aforesaid quality of things becomes evident,

> just as you perceive the speed at which a ship is going only when looking at the motionless shore, not when looking into the ship itself.
> (2001: §138, emphasis added).

Additionally, Schopenhauer can also be heard speaking to the un-pre-think-able ground of nature (as the future and abyss), while invoking the same notion of nobility-in-the-face of fate highlighted above by Schelling: "No one knows what forces for suffering and acting he has within himself until an occasion puts them into operation." (Ibid: §332).

{4} In conclusion, we should be able to recognize that all of the principles of existentialism can be found in Schelling's *Romantische Naturphilosophie* and Schopenhauer's philosophy of life. Both of them critique Hegel's philosophy as being, or at least resulting in, nihilism. What is more, both of them conceive of nature in such a way that they both affirm (1) the mystery of existence, that is, the principle of existential philosophy that existence exceeds consciousness. They both affirm (2) the transcendental freedom of the existing individual to make one's own choices and determine the meaning of one's own experience and life. As transcendental philosophers, they both affirm (3) the mineness of existence and consider it more primordial than the world one represents to one's self. They both affirm (4) the existential value and necessity of suffering for the sake of actualizing one's personality and, thereby, awareness of transcendental be-ing.

Thus, they also both – as noted explicitly in the above examples – recognize the capacity of the existing individual to cultivate a style of dwelling in regard to the reality of be-ing-in-time. That is to say, both affirm an ethic of nobility that encompasses (5) authenticity, (6) integrity, and (7) sincerity.

The "Philosophical Genealogy" Answer

§3 Kierkegaard, *The Sickness Unto Death*: The Leap of Faith to Become Who You Are

This section is divided into the following sub-sections: {1} the major interpretations of Søren Kierkegaard's (1813-1855) philosophizing, and the writings examined to bring forth his existential philosophy; {2} Kierkegaard's characterization of the principles of existentialism; {3} Kierkegaard on worldliness, self-actualization, and the inauthentic as "the demonic"; {4} Kierkegaard on death and the Knight of Faith.

{1} Kierkegaard is not an easy thinker to understand. There seems to have developed two standard approaches to his philosophy. The first, which is favored by those primarily interested in his critical relation to Christianity, takes *Fear & Trembling* (1843) to be exemplary of his philosophy and then goes on to emphasize *Concluding Unscientific Postscript to Philosophical Fragments* (1846).

The second, which is favored by those primarily interested in his existential philosophy, centers on his *The Concept of Anxiety* (1844), aka *The Concept of Dread*, and *The Sickness Unto Death* (1849) to characterize and thematize his work and, then, looks to writings such as *The Concept of Irony/Schelling Lecture Notes* (1841), *Either/Or* (1843), *Stages on Life's Way* (1845), and *Concluding Unscientific Postscript to Philosophical Fragments* (1846) to understand its profundity.

It has become, of course, standard to refer to Kierkegaard as "an existentialist." As there is nothing controversial about this, we can begin immediately illustrating his exemplary instantiation of the principles of existentialism. As noted throughout this book, these principles, ultimately, come from the philosophy of Kierkegaard's favorite philosopher, that is, Kant's transcendental philosophy.

{2} Now, there is a passage from Kierkegaard's *The Concept of Anxiety* that is so powerful we should consider it here in its totality, even though it is quite lengthy. I have added numbers to the passage to help facilitate discussion.

[1] Anxiety may be compared with dizziness. [2] He whose eye happens to look down into the yawning abyss becomes dizzy. But what is the reason for this? It is just as much in his own eye as in the abyss, for suppose he had not looked down. [3] Hence, anxiety is the dizziness of freedom, which emerges when the spirit wants to posit the synthesis and freedom looks down into its own possibility, laying hold of finiteness to support itself. Freedom succumbs in this dizziness. Further than this, psychology cannot, and will not, go. [4] In that very moment everything is changed, and freedom, when it again rises, sees that it is guilty. Between these two moments lies the leap, which no science has explained and which no science can explain. [5] He who becomes guilty in anxiety becomes as ambiguously guilty as it is possible to become... Psychologically speaking, the fall into sin always takes place in weakness. But anxiety is of all things the most selfish, and no concrete expression of freedom is as selfish as the possibility of every concretion. This again is the overwhelming factor that determines the individual's ambiguous relation, sympathetic and antipathetic. In anxiety there is the selfish infinity of possibility, which does not tempt like

> a choice but ensnaringly disquiets with its sweet anxiousness. (1981: 61).

First, the association of anxiety with dizziness becomes a standard for existentialism and is echoed by Heidegger and the French Existentialists. Second, Kierkegaard's linking of this dizziness with the abyss places all of these concepts in a direct trajectory from Kant through Schelling and Schopenhauer. Though there are plenty of other places where Kierkegaard instantiates the first two principles of existentialism, the points already enumerated here from the above passage may also be understood as indicating Kierkegaard's affirmation of the first two principles of existentialism.

Third, Kierkegaard positions dizziness here in terms of freedom and spirit "laying hold of finiteness to support itself." There is a lot here to unpack. On the one hand, (a) spirit in its freedom is dizzied by the immensity of possibility, and the concept of care is also invoked here with the idea of "supporting itself." In other words, spirit is concerned to support itself. On the other hand, Kierkegaard is characterizing anxiety as a natural and necessary aspect of the ontology of the existing individual. This is the case, since the existing individual is ontologically free and necessarily will die. Thus, (b) the existing individual will necessarily be anxious.

Hence, notice all of the aspects of existence considered thus far by Kierkegaard in this passage constitute a universal existential philosophy in that the aspects discussed all necessarily apply to each existing individual. It is the nature of every existing individual to be free and to either survive by actualizing some possible way to support itself or die (b). When the existing individual looks at its future it becomes anxious facing the abyss of possible ways its existence might be (a).

Fourth, then, Kierkegaard mentions here "the leap" between two moments.[19] The one moment is the moment in which spirit's freedom is dizzyied, and the other moment is the moment in which an awareness arises that the dizziness of freedom is a sign that freedom is "guilty." In this way, anxiety reveals guilt as a fallen/worldly mode of freedom and the revelation itself as a communication of conscience. That is to say, if spirit rises from the abyss by acknowledging its guilt in relation to the world, then it has made a leap – what Kierkegaard will elsewhere, of course, call a "leap of faith" – into a different relation between freedom and worldliness for spirit.

Fifth, Kierkegaard invokes the ideas of ambiguity and mineness. The experience is ambiguous for the existing individual because it is in terms of possibility, not actuality, that the individual is guilty. If it were actuality, then the guilt would not be ambiguous. This is why Heidegger says of the "call of conscience" that it is silent, and Nietzsche said of conscience, "What does your conscience say? – 'You shall become the person you are.'" That is to say, the revelation brought forth by conscience through the necessity of freedom's anxiety calls it toward its transcendental dimension to reduce the ambiguity in which it is submerged. Thus, the way out of this anxiety/dread for freedom is spirit's self-actualization.

In Kantian terms, this self-actualization manifests when the existing individual rises to the point of view of personality. As noted previously, this means rising from the ambiguity of freedom's relation to possibilities from the points of view of animality or humanity. Kierkegaard's way of characterizing this

---

[19] Keep in mind "spirit" for Kierkegaard refers to transcendental be-ing in Kant.

The "Philosophical Genealogy" Answer

appears in his *Either/Or* (1843), *Stages on Life's Way* (1845), *Concluding Unscientific Postscript to Philosophical Fragments* (1846), and *The Sickness Unto Death* (1849). For simplicity's sake, the distinction between "the demonic" versus "the religious" may be understood as covering animality and humanity versus personality or the worldly versus the Christian or the herd versus the artist (Nietzsche) the inauthentic versus the authentic (Heidegger) or bad faith versus good faith (Sartre).

It is important to notice that the movement is seamless. That is to say, Kierkegaard is absolutely doing ontology here. He is characterizing *necessary aspects of existence*. Every existing individual, simply by existing, will find its freedom involved in these various modes, moods, and points of view. Thus, existentialism characterizes freedom's *relation* to possibilities in terms of anxiety and one's point of view in terms of the context for determining and understanding possibilities; existentialism does not characterize freedom in terms of the content of the possibilities.

{3} According to Kierkegaard, then, "The demonic is, of course, not dependent upon the variety of the intellectual content but upon the relation of freedom to the given content" (1981: 137-8). As a result, freedom can fall into a demonic relation to the content of experience, and anticipating Heidegger's elucidation of fallenness in *Being & Time* by almost a century, Kierkegaard noted

> the demonic is able to express itself [an intellectual attitude toward what is given in experience] as indolence that postpones thinking, as curiosity that never becomes more than curiosity, as dishonest self-deception, as

> effeminate weakness that constantly relies on others, as superior negligence, as stupid busyness... (1981: 138).

For Kierkegaard, freedom falls into the world, and it is the truth that sets freedom free from anxiety. Yet, truth sets freedom free by being the work of freedom, that is, insofar as truth is that which freedom works to bring forth.

On the one hand, this truth is the existing individual's revelation that it is transcendental spirit. On the other hand, this is the place to recall Kierkegaard's celebrated journal entry:

> What I really need is to get clear about is what I must do, not what I must know, except insofar as knowledge must precede every act. What matters is to find a purpose ... the crucial thing is to find a truth which is truth for me, to find the idea for which I am willing to live and die. (*Journal 1*: entry, 08/01/1835).

For it is the finding of that for which I am willing to live and die that reduces the ambiguity and brings freedom into a relation to be-ing that can be characterized in terms of authenticity, integrity, and sincerity.

Kierkegaard also expressed this in terms of mineness in the mode of personality: "every life-view that has a condition outside itself is despair." (2013: 235). Just as "the greatest thing is not to be this or that but to be oneself..." (2013: 177), so too, one is to own one's death by choosing one's life; this brings mineness to completion as freedom chooses and commits to the truth of its finitude. Thus, "the question is whether a person will in the deepest sense acknowledge the truth, will allow it to permeate his whole being, will accept all its consequences, and not have an emergency hiding place for himself." (1981: 138).

The "Philosophical Genealogy" Answer

{4} Kierkegaard explicitly understood this in terms of what Heidegger would later call a be-ing-toward-death. Kierkegaard declared: "Therefore, death first! You must first die to every merely earthly hope, to every merely human confidence..." (2015: 77). This is, of course, a call *to* the transcendental (personal) point of view and away from the points of view of subjectivity (hedonism) and objectivity (i.e., animality and humanity). For,

> Who has not heard how one day, sometimes one hour, gained infinite worth because death made time dear! Death is able to do this, but with the thought of death the earnest person is able to create a scarcity so that the year and the day receive infinite worth... (1990: 84).

Notice just as earnestness means seriousness and sincerity, so too this quote indicates an authenticity regarding the seriousness of one's mineness over worldliness and a sincerity regarding finitude; notice this quote also indicates an integrity across time, that is, an integrity regarding be-ing-in-time.

Thus, we can see that Kierkegaard's "four aspects to earnestness [seriousness and sincerity] toward death" and his "stages along life's way" fit into the discussion we just concluded in the following way. Consider, the four aspects of Kierkegaard's earnestness toward death: (1) Owning one's death; (2) Affirming the truth of death's inevitability; (3) Affirming the uncertainty of death's arrival; (4) Managing the fear of death. (cf. Stokes and Buben, 2011). Most important for existentialism is "owning one's death."

This means we are not to think about death in general, but, rather, as in Kierkegaard's discourse "At a Graveside," we are to think about our actual death. Given how you live, what death might actually be yours? What might it look like? This is intended to intensify life by showing that in order to truthfully think about your way of living it must be seen in terms of finitude. This is what Kierkegaard referred to in his discourse "Purity of Heart," that is, "Purity of heart is to will one thing."

Perhaps we have not fully chosen the path we are on, until we avowedly choose to die on it. It is like saying: I choose to do this, and when its death comes, that will be *my* death. I own this death. It is not something from which to run away. It is mine. The other aspects of earnestness (seriousness and sincerity) toward death are, ultimately, in the service of coming to own one's death.

For, we affirm the truth of death's inevitability when we recognize that our worldly existence is finite. We affirm the uncertainty of death's arrival by sincerely relating to how we choose to spend each moment on our path. Everything that is done is done in the light of death. Knowing I only have so much time, I choose to spend it this way. And, lastly, this is not a fear-of-death-based attitude. We are not running to or from death. We are choosing to live our life – keeping in mind that mind-external reality and the future are ultimately mysterious. In this way, we own our death and our life.

Just as the "sickness unto death," according to Kierkegaard, is "constantly dying without being able to die," so too by owning our death we become who we are. Notice how this aligns with Kierkegaard's stages of life: the Aesthetic (animality), the Knight of Infinite Resignation (humanity), and the Knight of Faith (personality).

For Kierkegaard, when one is be-ing the Knight of Faith: "the soul comes to be alone in the whole world..." (2014: 177). And, the soul's self-relation is not in "bad faith." As Kierkegaard noted in his *Concluding Unscientific Postscript to Philosophical Fragments*, "Faith is the objective uncertainty with the repulsion of the absurd, held fast in the passion of inwardness" (1992: 610-1). Just as the first part signals the transcendental beyond the subjective and objective, the second part signals the absurdity of worldliness, and the third part points to the passion to become who one is that motivates the Knight's leap of Faith.

In conclusion, we should be able to recognize that Kierkegaard's philosophy expressed all of the principles of existentialism and in terms of a spiritual ontology. That is to say, Kierkegaard, rightly, considered these principles necessary features of transcendental be-ing individuated as an existing person in the world. The emphasis on personal commitment and appropriating freedom's truth of finitude (owning one's death) represents Kierkegaard's instantiation of his existential critique – existentialism's critique – of Hegel's nihilisms.

§4 Nietzsche, *Twilight of the Idols*: The Fatal Joy of Existing

I have written so much regarding the philosophy of Friedrich Nietzsche (1844-1900) my goal, here, is to remain as succinct as possible. This section contains passages from my *Full Throttle Heart: The Rapture & Ecstasy of Nietzsche's Dionysian Worldview* (2019). For a more in-depth discussion of Nietzsche's philosophy, I encourage you to read that book.

This section is divided into the following sub-sections: {1} the phases of Nietzsche's philosophizing; {2} Nietzsche's characterization of the constitutional principles of existentialism; {3} Nietzsche's characterization of the actualization principles of existentialism; {4} Nietzsche's criticism of the concept of consciousness; {5} Nietzsche on integrity, sincerity, and the "free death."

{1} It is helpful to understand the history of Nietzsche's philosophy in terms of its three phases. Early Phase: *The Birth of Tragedy* to *The Joyful Quest* (1872-1882), Middle Phase: *Thus Spoke Zarathustra* to *Toward the Genealogy of Morality* (1883-1887), and Late Phase: *Twilight of the Idols* to *The Will-to-Power* (1888). The following three paragraphs come from pages 8-9 of *Full Throttle Heart* (2019).

The "Early" or "First Phase" of Nietzsche's philosophy runs from the publication of the first edition of *The Birth of Tragedy* in 1872 to 1882 with the publication of the first edition of *Die fröhliche Wissenschaft*, which has been various translated as: *The Joyful Wisdom*, *The Cheerful Science*, *The Gay Science*, or *The Joyful Quest*.

This first decade of Nietzsche's philosophical writings includes his *Untimely Meditations*, sometimes translated as *Thoughts out of Season*: though Nietzsche's plan was to write thirteen essays, in the end these "meditations" (spanning from 1873-1876) total only four: "David Strauss: the Confessor and Writer," "On the Use and Abuse of History for Life," "Schopenhauer as Educator," and "Richard Wagner in Bayreuth."

The rest of the decade of the Early Phase in the history of Nietzsche's philosophical writings is filled by what is known as the "Free Spirit Trilogy" of *Human, All too Human* (1878), *The Dawn* (1881), sometimes translated as *Daybreak*, and the first edition of *The Joyful Quest* (1882). It was in the first edition of *The Joyful Quest* that Nietzsche first expressed his "Eureka!" idea of "the Eternal Return." Thus, this book – and this revelation – opened a new phase in Nietzsche's philosophical history.

The "Philosophical Genealogy" Answer

The following three paragraphs also come from *Full Throttle Heart* (2019), the first two paragraphs from page 11 and the third from page 12.

Nietzsche's second or "Middle Phase" begins with *Thus Spoke Zarathustra* (1883-5) and concludes with *Toward the Genealogy of Morality* (1883-7). Also, this phase is characterized by the publication of the second edition of *The Joyful Quest* (1887). Finally, it was in this phase that Nietzsche began self-publishing his books, starting with *Beyond Good & Evil* (1886). Thus, over half of Nietzsche's books were self-published.

To help orient us in regard to the history of Nietzsche's concepts, it was during this phase that Nietzsche developed the following philosophical ideas: (1) the Eternal Return, (2) the *Übermensch*, (3) Perspectivism, and (4) *Amor Fati*.

The Late Phase of Nietzsche's philosophy is popularly remembered as the phase in which Christianity is most explicitly criticized, and the paroxysmal characterization of this phase is supported by highlighting the explosiveness with which he published in the year 1888, before his collapse in January of 1889. These writings include: *The Case of Wagner* (1888), *Twilight of the Idols* (1888), *The Anti-Christ* (1888), sometimes translated as *The Anti-Christian*, his autobiographical *Ecce Homo* (1888), *Nietzsche contra Wagner* (1888), and the *Unpublished Writings*, also known as *The Will to Power*.

Lastly, by way of introduction to Nietzsche's existential philosophy, we should consider the question of whether Nietzsche was aware of Kierkegaard's philosophy. This is one of my favorite insights about Nietzsche, because throughout my schooling in philosophy I was told that Nietzsche was neither aware of Kierkegaard's work nor aware of Kierkegaard's existence; however, it turns out that Nietzsche was reading excerpts from, and secondary sources specifically on, Kierkegaard's idea of *repetition* at the time when the idea of the Eternal Return "dawned" on him![20,21]

Now, we will consider the constitutional principles of existentialism together, since the first three principles – mystery, mineness, and freedom – come tangled together in Nietzsche's idea of the Dionysian *World*-view. Nietzsche also referred to this in his Late Phase as Will-to-Power. Of course, these ideas refer us to the transcendental dimension.

{2} We should consider two passages from Nietzsche, so that we can understand how he is navigating the structures of Kant's transcendental philosophy and articulating his expression of the framework and principles of existentialism. First, from *The Birth of Tragedy*, §1,

> In song and in dance man expresses himself as a member of a higher community; he has forgotten how to walk and speak and is on the way toward flying into the air, dancing. His very gestures express enchantment. ... *He is no longer an artist, he has become a work of art*

---

[20] We know for certain – based on what Nietzsche himself said in his letters – exactly when and exactly what Nietzsche read regarding Kierkegaard. For example, in a February 19, 1888 letter to his friend Georg Brandes in Copenhagen, Nietzsche wrote: "For my next trip to Germany, I have decided to study the psychological problem of Kierkegaard and to *renew* [emphasis added] my acquaintance with your older literature." (cf. Scalambrino, 2019: 41-42).

[21] The sources for the Kierkegaard-Nietzsche connection are: J. Kellenberger's (1997) *Kierkegaard and Nietzsche: Faith and Eternal Acceptance*; Wenche Marit Quist's (2005) "Nietzsche and Kierkegaard – Tracing Common Themes," and Thomas H. Brobjer's (2003) "Nietzsche's Knowledge of Kierkegaard." See the Bibliography below for the full citations.

The "Philosophical Genealogy" Answer

> [emphasis added]: in these paroxysms of ecstasy the artistic power of all nature reveals itself to the highest gratification of the primordial unity. The noblest clay, the most costly marble, man, is here kneaded and cut, and to the sound of the chisel strokes of the Dionysian world-artist rings out the cry of the Eleusinian mysteries ... 'Do you sense your Maker, *world*? [emphasis added]' (Nietzsche, 1967:37-38).

In regard to our question, "What is existentialism?" here Nietzsche tells us the relation between the "person" in Kant's three genera and transcendental be-ing is not determined by the principle of non-contradiction. That is to say, the relation is beyond either/or.

When we come to see this, then we recognize that the kind of individuation and individuality associated with the "human" level in Kant's three genera is not to be imported into our understanding of the "person" level. Nietzsche understood Kant's three genera (contexts for determining and understanding the meaning of existence) in terms of "orders of existence." Thus, the transcendental in Kant corresponds to the highest order of existence in Nietzsche. In fact, this is consistent across all of the existentialists.

What this accomplishes for Nietzsche is that it puts the existing individual into the appropriate relation with divinity – that is, into the proper relation (ontologically/constitutionally understood) with the transcendental dimension. By characterizing the "person" as "artist" and, then, claiming the artist has become a "work of art," he emphasizes the manner in which the life of the existing individual – the individual's experiences and *world* – are primordially an expression of divinity. Thus, fate enters the discussion and to exist is *fatal* in a deeper way.

Of course, for Nietzsche, the experience of these fatal events is the experience of divine affectivity. It is the experience of be-ing affected by the gods, and it is, *thereby*, joyful. This is Nietzsche's understanding of life and tragedy.

Second, whereas the above passage came from Nietzsche's early phase, the following comes from his late phase:

> And do you know what **'the world'** is to me? Shall I show it to you... This world: a monster of energy, without beginning, without end... enclosed by 'nothingness'... a play of forces... eternally changing... blessing itself as that which must return eternally, as a becoming that knows no satiety, no disgust, no weariness: this, my ***Dionysian* world of the eternally self-creating, the eternally self-destroying, this mystery world of the twofold ecstasy, my 'beyond good and evil,'** ... – do you want a *name* for this world? A *solution* for all its riddles? ... *This world is the* Wille zur Macht [*Will-to-Power/Create/Actualize*] – *and nothing besides!"* **And you yourselves are** also [an expression of] **this** *Wille zur Macht* – **and nothing besides!** (1969: §1067).

Juxtaposing this passage with the previous one from *The Birth of Tragedy* is especially powerful. Will-to-Power is Nietzsche's characterization of what – through Kant – we call the transcendental dimension. Some English translations have it as the Will-to-Actualize, and when we see it translated that way, then we can recognize the transcendental dimension as actualizing itself.

The "Philosophical Genealogy" Answer

On the one hand, notice that Nietzsche's characterization here is very much like Schelling's and Schopenhauer's understanding of the relation between the world experienced by the individual and Nature. On the other hand, it expresses the German Romantic (Novalis') realization and actualization of transcendental be-ing as an apotheosis. Put yet another way, Nietzsche has characterized the constitutional principles in terms of the principles of *actualization*.

What ground have we covered at this point? We have just seen that the mystery, mineness, and freedom of the existing individual are all tied together for Nietzsche in the Will-to-Actualize [*Wille-zur-Macht*].[22] In the above passage Nietzsche explicitly draws our attention to the mystery, and in the passage prior he explicitly draws our attention to his (what I call) "beyond either/or" characterization of mineness. Freedom is present in both of the passages in the sense of taking hold of one's own Will-to-Power.[23] And, "one's own" in the previous sentence should be understood as the mysterious mineness beyond either/or.

{3} Thus, what is left for the Nietzsche section of this chapter is to discuss: anxiety, authenticity, integrity, and sincerity. Just like the constitutional principles just discussed, all of these principles are also tied together in Nietzsche.

In regard to anxiety, authenticity, and integrity, then, we need to understand (of course) the Eternal Return and *Amor Fati*. Since, the latter was discussed in section Four of the

---

[22] Again, I present Nietzsche's philosophy with much more detail in the 2nd edition of *Full Throttle Heart*. I encourage anyone interested in Nietzsche to read that book.

[23] Those already familiar with Heidegger, will recognize how his notion of "ownmost potential" is exactly what we are seeing here in Nietzsche.

previous chapter (Ch. 2), we will discuss the former now. To do so, we will discuss (a) how to understand its name, (b) what does the Eternal Return mean, (c) how it functions as a kind of "test," and (d) how it connects with *Amor Fati*.

(a) Nietzsche scholars sometimes squabble over what to call the Eternal Return. For the purposes of this book, I'm not overly concerned with this issue; however, its brief presentation of the issue may be of value for readers: The Eternal Return is also sometimes called "the Eternal Return of the Same" and "the *Idea* of Eternal Recurrence." What is at stake here is the question of the repetition's ontological status. In other words, does it refer to an actual eternal repetition? Is that repetition of everything in the exact same way? Is it merely an idea that constitutes a kind of selection or test? Or, is it somehow more than just one of these options?

For the purpose of providing a kind of vision and awareness – or envisioning-awareness – of Nietzsche's Dionysian Worldview, I treat the Eternal Return as the characterization of Nature and as an existential test. It may also be helpful to briefly look at Nietzsche's German: "*die ewige Wiederkehr*." The term "*ewige*" may also be translated as "everlasting," and "*Wiederkehr*" may be seen as composed of two words: "again" and "turn."[24]

(b) What does "the Eternal Return" mean? When asked in isolation like this, I always invoke *The Joyful Quest* §341. The epigram there is titled: "The greatest weight." Nietzsche asks us to suppose some demon or daimon were to say to us:

---

[24] This should call to mind, for example, Heidegger's discussions of "the twisting free."

The "Philosophical Genealogy" Answer

> This life as you now live it and have lived it, you will have to live once more and innumerable times more; and there will be nothing new in it, but every pain and every joy and every thought and sigh and everything unutterably small or great in your life will have to return to you, all in the same succession and sequence... (Nietzsche, 1974, §341).

If one is simply asked what is the Eternal Return, that epigram tends to be the response.

Importantly, though, Nietzsche concludes the epigram with a question and a potential response to the question: "Would you not throw yourself down and gnash your teeth and curse the demon who spoke thus?" Notice how Nietzsche characterizes an alternative response: "Or have you once experienced a tremendous moment when you would have answered him: 'You are a god and never have I heard anything more divine.'" (Ibid).

It is in this way that the Eternal Return is discussed as a kind of test. Namely, how would you respond to it? The former response is supposed to be a herd response. It makes sense to call it this given the herd understanding of tragedy and suffering. The latter response is supposed to be the response that would come from the highest order of existence. Why? Because the revelation of divine presence is not lost on the childlike innocence of the highest order, and the point of view of the highest order affirms the divinity involved in the situation further insofar as it acknowledges the fatal identity of the revelation. I mean: if this divine revelation is informing you of your fate, then you will not be able to escape it.

(c) Nietzsche concludes the epigram by noting what may be thought of as a mantra of the highest order.

> If this thought gained possession of you, it would change you as you are or perhaps crush you. The question in each and every thing, 'Do you desire this once more and innumerable times more?' would lie upon your actions as the greatest weight. Or how well disposed would you have to become to yourself and to life to crave nothing more fervently than this ultimate eternal confirmation and seal? (Ibid).

In this way, the Eternal Return may be seen as a principle of selection or a kind of "test." Following Gilles Deleuze (1925-1995), I also refer to this as the "selective principle of Eternal Recurrence." The idea here is actually quite straightforward: how you respond to the idea of the Eternal Return reveals something about you, namely, the order of existence in which you dwell.

(d) Finally, how does the Eternal Return relate to fate? *Amor Fati*, as the goal of the joyful quest and sign of *apotheosis* points to the highest, transcendental, context for determining and understanding the meaning of life and, thereby, it also indicates the highest relation to the Eternal Return as a selective principle (or test). **When the response to the test is, sincerely, *Amor Fati*, then the individual is be-ing authentic, and traverses the Return with integrity**. As will be discussed in just a moment, it is through sincerity, then, that the existing individual sustains the *Amor Fati*-relation to the Eternal Return. Yet, first, we should consider how the apotheosis of actualization relates to the call of conscience, since that call is tied up with the anxiety of facing the Eternal Return.

Through the completion of the existing individual's "quest" to become who one is, one is able to experience the fatal joy of existing – *Amor Fati*. Consider,

The "Philosophical Genealogy" Answer

> **The genius of the heart** as that great mysterious one possesses it, the tempter god and born **pied-piper of consciences** whose voice **knows how to descend into the Underworld of every soul**... the genius of the heart which teaches the clumsy and too hasty hand to hesitate and grasp more delicately... the genius of the heart, from whose touch everyone goes away richer... not as though gratified or oppressed by the good things of others; but richer in himself, newer than before, broken open... full of hopes which as yet are without names, full of **a new will**... Of whom am I speaking? ... namely, no less a one than **the god Dionysus**... (BGE, §295).

This is Nietzsche's characterization of the Eternal Return of transcendental be-ing, and the conscience of the existing individual awakening to itself as authentic be-ing.

By focusing on the principle of integrity involved here, we can see that authentic transcendental be-ing corresponds to the non-nihilistic response to witnessing be-ing in the lower orders of existence. In other words, here is the place for Nietzsche's Master versus Slave mentality and morality. Think of it like this:

If transcendental be-ing is the most primordial dimension of an existing individual's be-ing, then non-authentic be-ing involves be-ing separated from "what it can do," or "its ownmost potential," or the consistent expression of Will-to-Power (and "consistent" means with integrity, thru sincerity).

Consider Deleuze's articulation from *Nietzsche & Philosophy* (1962), "reactive forces do not triumph by forming a superior force but by 'separating' active forces" (2006: 57).

Hence, "the words 'vile', 'ignoble', and 'slave' ... designate the state of reactive forces that place themselves on high and entice active force into a trap, replacing masters with slaves" (Ibid:57-58). In other words, whereas the lower orders of existence respond to the test of the Eternal Return in a "reactive" way, the "active" response is, of course, only possible by activating (actualizing) transcendental be-ing.

This is the case because it always already is the activity of transcendental be-ing. To try to not accept the fate of one's ownmost potential is to attempt to level the mystery of mineness and the reality of freedom. At bottom, integrity here should be understood as the integration of one's be-ing, the making whole of one's Will-to-Power across time – across the timespan of the Eternal Return. Interestingly, Nietzsche's transvaluation of all values in terms of what he called "the problem of consciousness" clarifies the actualization principles.

In Nietzsche's *The Joyful Quest*, he noted the following about the orders of existence.

> **What distinguishes higher human beings from the lower** is that the former see and hear immeasurably more, and see and hear more thoughtfully – and precisely this distinguishes human beings from animals, and the higher animals from the lower... Only **we have created** *the world that concerns man!* (1974, Bk IV: §301).

Further, at the level of the existing individual, Nietzsche formulated this insight as the "problem of consciousness."

> The problem of consciousness (more precisely, of becoming conscious of something) confronts us only when we begin to comprehend how we

could dispense with it... For we could think, feel, will, and remember, and we could also 'act' in every sense of that word, and yet none of all this would have to 'enter our consciousness'... The whole of life would be possible without, as it were, seeing itself in a mirror. (Ibid: §354).

{4} Lastly, then, Nietzsche provided his conclusion from these insights with the following passage:

> **My idea is**, as you see, **that consciousness does not really belong to man's individual existence but rather to his social or herd nature**; that, as follows from this, it has developed subtlety only insofar as this is required by social or herd utility... [Thus,] Our thoughts themselves are continually governed by the character of consciousness – by the 'genius of the species' that commands it – and translated back into the perspective of the herd. **Fundamentally, all our actions are altogether incomparably personal, unique, and infinitely individual; there is no doubt of that. But as soon as we translate them into consciousness *they no longer seem to be*.** (Ibid).

First, notice for Nietzsche, consciousness is a byproduct of inauthentic transcendental be-ing, it belongs to Kant's "human" context for determining and understanding the meaning of existence. Second, the problem Nietzsche is highlighting for us here is what I refer to as "the triumph of generality." In other words, from the point of view of the highest order of existence, everything is "person-al." Yet, it is to the herd's advantage for us to translate our personal experience into the general categories of consciousness, because then our experiences feel, and seem to be, more shared with others.

In other words, the presence in our minds of some meanings and some possible interpretations of reality may depend on the herd. This includes, of course, the style in which you philosophize, and *the way you talk to yourself*. On the one hand, Nietzsche uses this insight to show that some of the concerns referred to as "human" concerns are really herd-mentality concerns. Thus, according to Nietzsche, the authenticity, integrity, and sincerity of transcendental be-ing get lost in the "translation" of experience into consciousness.

On the other hand, Nietzsche suggests that the extent to which herd values are meaningful to you may reveal your "herd instinct." Yet, this is a tricky claim; it is tricky because it raises two deeper questions regarding Nietzsche's philosophy and its relation to its readers. First, supposing someone finds "herd instincts" in their psychological constitution, are they able to transcend the influence of these instincts as they navigate their existence? Second, would it even be *valuable* to transcend herd instincts and values?

In regard to the first deeper question, it seems as though Nietzsche believed that one can transcend the herd despite any herd instincts. Were this interpretation not correct, then his concern to articulate a "transvaluation of all values" would seem incoherent. In regard to the second deeper question, it seems to me that that's where things get person-al. No one can decide for you how you navigate your own existence – assuming you are in fact capable of person-hood. Ultimately, no one can make your choices for you; no one can face your existential tests for you; no one can die your death for you.

The "Philosophical Genealogy" Answer

{5} In order to show the way sincerity for Nietzsche figures into the integrity of authentic transcendental be-ing, I have reproduced Part II, Chapter 2, §34 from the 2nd edition of *Full Throttle Heart*. The title of that section is: "The Aesthetic Dimension of Divine Affectivity: What is the Difference between Romantic Irony and Insincerity?" After re-producing it here, I will provide a conclusion for this Nietzsche section:

To take some thing's dimensions is to measure it. If the metaphor with which the Enlightenment liked to think was "machine," Romanticism's is "life." The term "machine" comes with the implication of measurable moving parts, scientifically-precise predictions, and no mysterious "dimensions." Yet, the parts and depths of "life" strike us as uncountable, unfathomable, unpredictable, and, thereby, mysterious.

An "aesthetic dimension" refers to our sensory experience of life. That life exceeds our capacity to fully-experience it, given the limits of our sensory capacities, is a transcendental truth. Thus, on the one hand, it is neither subjective nor objective; rather, it is an insight gained by considering our limitations (cf. Nietsche, 1974, BK V: §354). Yet, on the other hand, it is true that there are both subjective and objective aspects to our sensory experiences. This means there are three aspects for us to consider regarding an aesthetic dimension.

The idea, then, is that in being affected by existence, we have three different ways to consider the aesthetic dimension that manifests. Most people will think we are talking about the subjective aspect of the aesthetic dimension; however, we are actually discussing the difference between the transcendental, on the one hand, and the subjective and objective, on the other. Further, we are taking the transcendental to be the most primordial of the three aspects, and, therefore, the subjective and objective aspects of the aesthetic dimension can be seen as the expressions of the transcendental within our sensory capacities. Thus, what we are discussing is beyond the objective/subjective distinction, contains them both, and is universal.

Now, we have discussed this already above, so we'll just mention here that the relation between the transcendental, on the one hand, and the subjective/objective on the other is the distinction between Dionysian-Play and Apollonian-Illusion, respectively. This is precisely why Nietzsche can call the Apollonian "illusory," because it cannot characterize the transcendental.

Importantly, then, in this context, when we use *either* the subjective *or* the objective to attempt to characterize the transcendental, there will always be some "irony" involved. This is a highly misunderstood insight, so let's get clear on it here. The distinction we need to come to understand is between irony and Romantic irony. Namely, both sarcasm and insincerity are forms of irony, because they are instances of language which negate what they actually say. In contrast, Romantic irony does not negate what it says; however, it does call what it says into question. *Voilà*. Hence, Apollonian representations of Dionysian-play are seen in the light of Romantic irony – it is in that way that they are ironic. This will help us think through Nietzsche's discussion of lucid dreaming.

i. The Joyful Quest, Book I, §54

The passage in question here comes from *Die fröhliche Wissenschaft*, Book I, §54. Here is Kaufman's translation:

> *The consciousness of appearance.* – How wonderful and new and yet how gruesome and

The "Philosophical Genealogy" Answer

> ironic I find my position vis-à-vis the whole of existence in the light of my insight! ...
> I have discovered for myself that the human and animal past, indeed the whole primal age and past of all sentient be[-]ing continues in me to invent, to love, to hate, and to infer. I suddenly woke up in the midst of this dream, only to the consciousness that I am dreaming and that I must go on dreaming lest I perish [from nihilism] ... What is appearance for me now? ...
> Appearance is for me that which lives and is effective and goes so far in its self-mockery that it makes me feel that this is appearance and will-o'-the-wisp and a dance of spirits and nothing more ...
> that among all these dreamers, I, too, who "know," am dancing **my** dance; that the knower is a means for prolonging the earthly dance and thus belongs to the masters of ceremony of existence; and that the sublime consistency and interrelatedness of all knowledge perhaps is and will be the highest means to *preserve* the universality of dreaming and the mutual comprehension of all dreamers and thus also *the continuation of the dream...*

With this passage Nietzsche affirms the mystery of existence; existence exceeds consciousness of existence, and, yet, we continue to be conscious of existence as it *appears* to us. On the one hand, his insight, then, is that awareness of the illusory – or Romantically-ironic – nature of the Apollonian does not change it. Yet, on the other, how are we to avoid believing that "nothing" is true or valuable, in light of such an insight? Nietzsche is explicit here; that is, waking *in* the dream does not wake us *from* the dream.

Thus, to affirm *life* is to affirm in a Romantically-ironic way, because we recognize the inevitably-illusory nature of appearance; whether we interpret the aesthetic dimension subjectively or objectively, the transcendental will always remain "higher." It is **Beyond** our mortal determinations of **Good & Evil**. And, yet, our existence is also transcendental in relation to our consciousness; and, thus, we are inextricably a part of the Dionysian-Play (i.e., the transcendental dimension).

This is precisely how the principle of sincerity is involved. Despite the irony that the transcendental dimension exceeds the subjective and objective dimensions, we continue to exist. Hence, in order to integrate authentic transcendental be-ing across time, we must *be* sincere regarding who we are, and that means in regard to our ownmost potential, and the way in which we traverse the Eternal Return as Will-to-Actualize.

As we will see in the next section, Heidegger (following Kierkegaard's "sickness unto death") explicitly characterized the resolute integrity sustained by sincerity in terms of be-ing-toward-death. That this is a part of Nietzsche's *Amor Fati*-relation to the Eternal Return should be clear from the above discussion; however, in case it isn't, the following should make Nietzsche's existential position more explicit. It is my translation of an excerpt from Nietzsche's epigram "On Free Death":

> Many die too late, and a few die too early... Die
> at the right time – thus teaches Zarathustra...
> Everyone considers dying important: but death
> is not yet a festival... I will show you the perfect

> death... He who dies this death, dies victoriously... The death I commend... is the free death that comes because you want it. And, when should you want it? Whoever has a goal and an heir wants death at the right time for his goal and heir. And, out of reverence for the goal and heir, such a person would no longer hang dry wreaths in the sanctuary of life... Free to die and free in death, able to say a holy No when the time for Yes has passed: thus, such a person knows how to die and how to live.

Here, Nietzsche commends the "free death," as opposed to – what we might call – the consumer-driven death that comes from attempting to live as long as one can. In fact, Nietzsche's characterization of "free death" may even be called "existentialist death" in that he is advocating that we sincerely exist authentically and with integrity.

To sincerely be who we are is to die the death that comes with that be-ing, not by attempting to dodge it simply for the sake of more life. If the Eternal Return is correct, there will be no shortage of life. For the existing individual to authentically be, they must be the death that comes with that be-ing. The nobility of the apotheosis of existential actualization affirms freedom and mineness, despite worldliness; "*The noble soul has reverence for itself*" (Nietzsche, 1989: 228).

§5 Heidegger, *Being & Time*: Be-ing in the Clearing of Care Thrown at Death

This section is divided into the following sub-sections: {1} the phases of Martin Heidegger's (1889-1976) philosophizing; {2} by way of the early phase of Heidegger's work, we will show his clarification of Kant's critique of Descartes; {3} we will consider a brief paraphrase of Heidegger's existential philosophy to prime us for the concluding part of this section of the chapter; {4} Heidegger's characterization of the constitutional and actualization principles of existentialism in *Being & Time*.

{1} The Table of Contents of the Harper Collins' anthology of Heidegger's *Basic Writings* (2008) illustrates the essential "pathmarks" of Heidegger's interests and thinking. There are four (4) such "phases": his early work emphasizing transcendental methodology as the existential-ontological analytic of *Da-Sein*; following *Being & Time* (1927), then, the *Kehre* or "turn" in Heidegger's thinking toward a second phase known as an ontology of events, marked by *Contributions to Philosophy* (written 1936-8); the third phase encompasses his thinking regarding technology and "the fourfold," marked by his *The Question Concerning Technology* (1954) and his lectures from the 1950's such as "Building Dwelling Thinking," and, finally, the fourth phase, encompasses his thinking regarding language and poetry, marked by his essays, "The Way to Language" (1959) and "The End of Philosophy and the Task of Thinking" (1964).

Still in the early phase, then, of Heidegger's thinking,[25] we find Heidegger's emphasis on the value of transcendental philosophy and methodology. Notable texts of this period regarding his clarification of Kant's (the transcendental) critique of Descartes appear in such works as: *Introduction to*

---

[25] Heidegger's most extended critique of Descartes can be found in the entire second Part of his *Introduction to Phenomenological Research*, §§16-44, there it participates in his criticizing of Husserl's phenomenology, especially its focus on "consciousness."

Phenomenological Research (1923-4) *The History of the Concept of Time* (1925), *Being & Time* (1927), *Phenomenological Interpretation of Kant's* Critique of Pure Reason (1927-8), and *Kant and the Problem of Metaphysics* (1929).

{2} Famously, in his *The History of the Concept of Time*, Heidegger re-works Descartes, redirecting the Cartesian desire for *certainty as a foundation for philosophizing* from Descartes' *cogito ergo sum* (the infamous "I think, therefore I am") to the existential *certainty of death*.

> the mode of be-ing of falling is also a covering up. It operates by way of a reinterpretation, not letting itself see what death is. But this still implies a constant seeing beforehand, so that what it conceals in it is its own be-ing. The inconspicuous concern of not thinking about death covers up a basic character in it, namely its *certainty*. This certainty is reinterpreted into uncertainty by means of the ambiguity of 'Everyone dies someday.' ... a statement about death which is really addressed to no one... (Heidegger, 1985: 316).

In contrast to the public "everyday" way of *not* concerning oneself with death, Heidegger describes the existential view of death as "my own possibility," noting: "This certainty, that 'I myself am in that I will die,' is *the basic certainty of Da-Sein* [being t/here] *itself.*" (Ibid).

In the very next sentence, then, Heidegger characterizes this certainty as an authentic "statement of *Da-Sein*, while *cogito sum* is only the semblance of such a statement." (Ibid: 317). Heidegger's clarification of this insight is worth considering:

> If such pointed formulations mean anything at all, then the appropriate statement pertaining to *Da-Sein* [be-ing t/here] in its be-ing would have to be *sum moribundus* ["I am in the throw of death"], *moribundus* not as someone gravely ill or wounded, but insofar as I am, I am *moribundus*. *The* moribundus *first gives the* sum *its sense.* (Heidegger, 1985: 317).

Another way to put this, which is, at least, consistent with all of Heidegger's early phase writings: "I am care thrown at death." In other words, my existence is characterized by that with which I concern myself, and, the essential aspect of that characterization is its temporariness/impermanence. Thus, I do not exist because I think, rather: the care that constitutes my be-ing here has not yet arrived at death, therefore I exist.

Finally, rounding out these thoughts, Heidegger provides a criticism of the (inauthentic) everyday leveling of concern for death, which is supposedly justified by the "indefinite" nature of death's arrival.

> The uncertainty with which *Da-Sein* [be-ing t/here] covers up its original certainty of be-ing is at the same time supported by the calculation and determination that, in any case, now – according to a general estimate, which is the way one tends to see things – death cannot be anticipated. One in a sense reckons that death can come anytime and, thereby, overlooks that this *indefiniteness*, whereby death can come at any moment, *belongs essentially to its certainty* [emphasis added]. For, this indefiniteness as to when death comes positively refers to the

possibility that it can come at any moment. (Ibid).

In other words, not knowing when death might come is not a reason to not be concerned with death. Rather, not knowing when death might come is a part of the revelation that death is coming.

{3} Now, on the one hand, before showing Heidegger's early thought ordered in terms of the principles of existentialism, a brief paraphrase of Heidegger's existential philosophy will be helpful to prime us, since some of the passages from *Being & Time* can be perplexing. Yet, on the other hand, as odd as it may sound to the ears of those only vaguely familiar with Heidegger, readers may find Heidegger's existential philosophy more straightforward than the existential philosophies of Kierkegaard, Nietzsche, and Sartre. This may be expected insofar as we understand Heidegger's project in *Being & Time* to be directed at methodically characterizing be-ing in terms of the temporality of existence, since, then, his vocabulary and phenomeno-logic provide a kind of science of existence. And, as a result, his philosophy may be seen as the scientific characterization of the existential philosophies of the others.

In either case, the following paraphrase should prove helpful. First, we need to recognize that the future is present in the now in terms of potentiality. If we are driving down a road, at each moment we could characterize our position in terms of our potential to reach our destination. Further, at each moment any number of factors could contribute to our potential to reach our destination, and, therefore, that potential would be in flux across time. Second, the end of our existing – that is to say, the end of this potentiality that I am in this moment – will arrive when we die. Thus, by existing, we are already in a process. The potency that we are is already in the process of arriving at its end.

Third, by becoming aware of this, we more fully actualize the potential to be free. That is to say, we can actualize a part of the potentiality that we are in terms of be-ing free to direct the potentiality more than we *can* originally. This is the spectrum book-ended by worldliness and mineness. Thus, we are /*Da-Sein*'s original Be-ing-in-the-world is/ characterized by "falling," since the process in which we may come to take hold of our own (mineness) potential is initially directed by the world, this means: our body, speech, and mind are directed by concerns of the environment and concerns of others, more than our own (mineness) concerns.

Fourth, just like in the philosophies of the other existentialists, when we begin to concern ourselves with death, we become anxious. That anxiety can, then, be used as fuel for us to push away environmental concerns and the concerns of others. For example, I decided to not attend a Koan study today, because I want to finish this book.

Fifth, then, when we begin to resist having our time squandered, a number of things begin to enter our awareness. We become more authentically ourselves because we have taken hold of our potentiality (which, of course, includes the environment in which we find ourselves and the presence of others) in our own way. In fact, what Heidegger calls *Da-Sein*'s potentiality for be-ing-a-whole also begins to actualize. In other words, we begin to experience ourselves, in relation to the passing of time, differently from when we had not taken hold of our potentiality by realizing our freedom.

This may be the most fascinating aspect of existentialism. Of course, in Kierkegaard's this is be-ing *one*'s

The "Philosophical Genealogy" Answer

self; where we are in Nietzsche's philosophy would be *Amor Fati*; yet, Heidegger's "be-ing-a-whole" explicitly highlights how integrity and sincerity come to light as we begin to be more authentically. That is to say, our experience of be-ing-in-time-as-a-whole shows us that integrity is default, rather than something adjunct. Our authentic be-ing is *integrated* across the time of our existence. It is only due to the influence of the world (which includes others) that we lose sight of our own wholeness and struggle to integrate various aspects of our be-ing into our be-ing-in-time-as-a-whole.[26]

Finally, it seems the actualization principles of existentialism function in a kind of "hermeneutic circle," at least, for Heidegger, since the way in which we are able to maintain our authenticity and integrity is by maintaining our sincerity in regard to the *mystery* of our death. By living in the light of (my own) death, we *can* resist falling into the concerns of worldliness.

The above seven (7) paragraphs, then, constitute a priming for what follows. This priming touched on each of the seven principles of existentialism and provided some initial clarity regarding Heidegger's vocabulary. However, again, by now I believe readers should be comfortable with terms such as "falling," "Be-ing-in-the-world," "mineness," and so on. The remainder of this section of the chapter will consider a number of passages, primarily from *Being & Time* (1927), to illustrate how Heidegger's existential philosophy instantiates the principles with which we provided the archaeological answer to the question, "What is existentialism?"

---

[26] Though, admittedly, there is controversy regarding how to interpret it, here might be the place to make note of Sartre's oft-quoted insight – from his play *No Exit* – that "Hell is other people" (1989).

{4} To begin with mystery: As evidenced by the "indefiniteness" that is part of its essence, death is a mystery for Heidegger. Here is a passage from *Being & Time*:

> As potentiality-for-Being, *Da-Sein* [be-ing t/here] cannot surpass the possibility of death. Death is the possibility of the absolute impossibility of *Da-Sein* [be-ing t/here]. Thus, death reveals itself as that possibility which is one's ownmost, non-relational, and unsurpassable. As such, death is something *distinctively* impending. Its existential possibility is based on the fact that *Da-Sein* is essentially disclosed to itself, and disclosed, indeed, as ahead-of-itself. This item in the structure of care has its most primordial concretion in Be-ing-toward-death. (294, H 250).

Heidegger's other way of characterizing the mystery of existence is in terms of "Be-ing-along-side" the world.

> Heidegger explicated this idea as "'Be-ing alongside' the world in the sense of being absorbed in the world" (1962: 80, H. 54). For Heidegger, the principle of mystery is intimately related to what may be understood as a spectrum spanning worldliness and mineness. Of course, this is (as noted in our priming above) also intimately related to the principle of freedom in that the everyday determination and understanding of *Da-Sein* is in terms of worldliness.

> The concept of 'facticity' implies that an entity 'within-the-world' has Be-ing-in-the-world in such a way that it can understand itself as bound up in its 'destiny' with the Be-ing of those entities which it encounters within its own world. (1962: 82, H. 56).

Thus, it is in terms of pulling back *from* worldliness *toward* mineness that allows one to actualize the potential to take hold of their own potential.

Next, we will see how Heidegger articulated anxiety in terms of Kierkegaard's stages along life's way, the three orders of existence in Nietzsche or the predispositions to the good in Kant. We have also been referring to this structure as the three contexts for determining and understanding the meaning of life. The basic idea in *Being & Time* is that because individuals are absorbed in worldliness, anxiety reveals what Heidegger calls one's "guilt" in regard to having fallen into a world.

This can be understood, if we consider how one can be guilty of handing over one's freedom. For, notice that when one hands over one's freedom, the question naturally arises: What is it that we find more valuable than salvation or liberation, or, in other words, our freedom? Thus, anxiety and guilt show freedom and mineness are more primordial than worldliness. Further, the condition for the possibility of the experience of guilt is a conscience.

As we will eventually see, Heidegger articulated what he, famously, came to refer to as "the call of conscience." Ontologically speaking, it refers to a call that comes from authentic be-ing calling out to fallen Be-ing-in-the-world. Inauthentic, fallen, be-ing is guilty of be-ing separated from its ownmost potential.

> Thrownness into death reveals itself to *Da-Sein* [be-ing t/here] in a more primordial and impressive manner in that attunement [*Befindlichkeit*] which we have called "anxiety." Anxiety in the face of death is anxiety "in the face of" that potentiality-for-Be-ing which is

> one's ownmost, non-relational, and unsurpassable. *That in the face of which one has anxiety is Being-in-the-world itself* [emphasis added]. That about which one has this anxiety is simply *Da-Sein's* [be-ing t/here's] potentiality-for-Be-ing. Anxiety in the face of death must not be confused with fear in the face of one's demise. This anxiety is not an accidental or random mood of "weakness" in some individual; but, as a basic attunement of *Da-Sein* [be-ing t/here], it amounts to the disclosedness of the fact that *Da-Sein* [be-ing t/here] exists as thrown Be-ing toward its end. (1962: 295; H 251).

This is how anxiety can lead to the revelation of one's Be-ing-toward-death and awaken their Be-ing-a-whole.

In case that isn't enough to justify the claim that anxiety leads one back to the primordiality of mineness and freedom, then consider the following.

> Anxiety individualizes *Da-Sein* [be-ing t/here] for its ownmost Be-ing-in-the-world, which as something that understands, projects itself essentially upon possibilities. Therefore, with that which it is anxious about, anxiety discloses *Da-Sein* [be-ing t/here] as *Be-ing-possible*, and indeed as the only kind of thing which it can be of its own accord as something individualized in individualization. (1962: 232, H. 187-8).

It is just as we noted above, then, the existential view of death leads to the revelation of one's freedom. Thus, we have considered the principle of mystery in Heidegger in terms of death as the mystery of freedom and the mystery of mineness as "be-ing-alongside" the world.

Now, though the term "mineness," as noted in the archaeological answer above, comes from Immanuel Kant's *Critique of Pure Reason*, it is safe to say that Heidegger popularized it as a standard term. Here is the passage quoted most often:

> Because *Da-Sein* [be-ing t/here] has *in each case mineness*, one must always use a *personal* pronoun when one addresses it: 'I am,' 'you are.' Furthermore, in each case *Da-Sein* [be-ing t/here] has always made some sort of decision as to the way in which it is in each case mine. (Heidegger, 1962: 68, H. 42).

Just a bit after the above passage, Heidegger provided the following passage clarifying mineness as along a spectrum of possibility.

> That entity which in its Being has this very Being as an issue, comports itself toward its Being as its ownmost possibility. In each case *Da-Sein* [be-ing t/here] *is* its possibility, and it 'has' this possibility, but not just as a property... And because *Da-Sein* [be-ing t/here] is in each case essentially its own possibility, it *can*, in its very Being, 'choose' itself and win itself; it can also lose itself and never win itself; or only 'seem' to do so. But only insofar as it is essentially something which can be *authentic* – that is, something of its own – can it have lost itself and not yet won itself. (1962: 68, H. 42-3).

Hence, Heidegger discussed what I am calling the principles of existentialism, and he even understood their grouping in terms of the constitutive principles and the actualizing principles. Though, he, of course, did not refer to his own discourse in terms of these principles.

The following two passages show that Heidegger named the extreme points of the spectrum spanning mineness and worldliness in terms of authentic and inauthentic. First in terms of mineness,

> *Da-Sein* [be-ing t/here] is an entity which, in its very Being, comports itself understandingly toward that Being. In saying this, we are calling attention to the formal concept of existence. *Da-Sein* [be-ing t/here] exists. Furthermore, *Da-Sein* is an entity which in each case I myself am. Mineness belongs to any existent *Da-Sein* [be-ing t/here], and belongs to it *as the condition which makes authenticity and inauthenticity possible* [emphasis added]. In each case *Da-Sein* [be-ing t/here] exists in one or the other of these two modes, or else it is modally undifferentiated.

Next, then, in terms of worldliness.

> But these are both ways [be-ing authentic and be-ing inauthentic] in which *Da-Sein's* Be-ing takes on a definite character, and they must be seen and understood ... as grounded upon that state of Being which we have called "*Be-ing-in-the-world.*" An interpretation of this **constitutive** state is needed if we are to set up our analytic of *Da-Sein* [be-ing t/here] correctly. (Heidegger, 1962: 78, H. 53).

The "Philosophical Genealogy" Answer

Finally, the next passage shows Heidegger associated authentic be-ing with not just mineness, but also with freedom.

> Anxiety makes manifest in *Da-Sein* [be-ing t/here] its *Be-ing toward* its ownmost potentiality-for-be-ing – that is, its *Be-ing free for* the freedom of choosing itself and taking hold of itself. Anxiety brings *Da-Sein* [be-ing t/here] face to face with its *Be-ing free for* the authenticity of its Be-ing... (1962: 232, H. 188).

As noted in the paraphrase-priming part of this section, we become anxious due to our position between mineness and worldliness, and it is our freedom that is at stake. Thus, we feel guilty even if we are not fully aware of our fallenness, and the call of conscience reaches us in the world calling us back to the freedom of our mineness in the face of the mystery of death.

It is at this point in the framework of existentialism that Heidegger's terminology is celebrated. For, it is in regard to the call of conscience and worldliness that Heidegger's vocabulary has become the scientific standard: anxiety, anticipation, resoluteness, and the authenticity of Be-ing-a-whole. Evidencing all the claims we just made, then, according to Heidegger: "Conscience summons *Da-Sein's* [be-ing t/here] Self from its lostness in the 'they.'" (1962: 319, H. 274), and *"In conscience Da-Sein* [be-ing t/here] *calls itself."* (1962: 320, H. 275). "When Kant represented the conscience as a 'court of justice' and made this the basic guiding idea in his Interpretation of it, he did not do so by accident" (1962: 339, H. 293).

When we are "lost" in "the they" our potentiality is divided against itself, just like Deleuze's description of masters versus slaves in Nietzsche's characterology. The inauthenticity of fallenness in the world is a *choice*.

> 'It' calls, against our expectations and even against our will. On the other hand, the call undoubtedly does not come from someone else who is with me in the world. The call comes *from* me and yet *from beyond me.* (1962: 320, H. 275).

It is the individual as transcendental be-ing who calls to the individual fallen into the world. It communicates in terms of anxiety, alienation (not-at-homeness) and guilt, and mystery and death.

Because the individual's potentiality is already fallen in the world, the individual becomes aware of its own be-ing as cast into a situation; this is very much like the metaphor of having been dealt a hand of cards by fate.

> As something thrown, *Da-Sein* [be-ing t/here] has been thrown *into existence.* It exists as an entity which has to be as it is and as it can be... The thrownness of this entity belongs to the disclosedness of the 'there' and reveals itself constantly in its current attunement. This attunement brings *Da-Sein* [be-ing t/here], more or less explicitly and authentically, face to face with the fact 'that it is, and that it has to be something with a potentiality-for-Be-ing as the entity which it is.' (1962: 321, H. 276).

This also explains why worldly identity or the types of good associated with animality or humanity fail to reduce existential anxiety.[27]

---

[27] Depending on context, I am using Stambaugh's translation of *Befindlichkeit* as "attunement" over M&R's "state-of-mind." State-of-mind sounds too mental and static. And, "attunement" can carry the

The "Philosophical Genealogy" Answer

> In the face of its thrownness *Da-Sein* [be-ing t/here] flees to the relief which comes with the supposed freedom of the they-self. This fleeing has been described as a fleeing in the face of the uncanniness which is basically determinative for individualized Be-ing-in-the-world. Uncanniness reveals itself authentically in the basic attunement of anxiety; and, as the most elemental way in which thrown *Da-Sein* [be-ing t/here] is disclosed, it puts *Da-Sein's* [be-ing t/here] Be-ing-in-the-world face to face with the 'nothing' of the world; in the face of this 'nothing,' *Da-Sein* [be-ing t/here] is anxious with anxiety about its ownmost potentiality-for-Be-ing. (1962: 321, H. 276).

It also seems clear that Heidegger valued mineness over worldliness in his description of how we cannot be "at home" in the modes of animality or humanity. "The caller is *Da-Sein* [be-ing t/here] in its uncanniness: primordial, thrown Be-ing-in-the-world as the 'not-at-home' – the bare 'that-it-is' in the 'nothing' of the world. The caller is unfamiliar to the everyday they-self; it is something like an *alien* voice." (1962: 321, H. 277). Heidegger even went so far as to characterize *the world* as "nothing."

The following two passages help clarify anxiety in regard to the mystery of thrownness, Be-ing-alongside the world, and why we say that be-ing is care thrown at death.

---

weight of characterizing multiple positions on the spectrum of the individual's relation to worldliness. For example, the existing individual can be attuned to the *Umwelt*/environment, the *Mitwelt*/world of others, or the *Selbstwelt*/mineness, which actualizes authentic be-ing.

> Conscience manifests itself as the call of care: the caller is *Da-Sein* [be-ing t/here], which, in its thrownness... is anxious about its potentiality-for-Be-ing. The one to whom the appeal is made is this very same *Da-Sein* [be-ing t/here], summoned to its ownmost potentiality-for-Being (ahead of itself ...) *Da-Sein* [be-ing t/here] is falling into the 'they' (in Be-ing-already-alongside the world of its concern), and it is summoned out of this falling by the ... call of conscience (1962: 322, H. 277-8).

Further, "*Da-Sein's* [be-ing t/here's] Be-ing is care. It comprises in itself facticity (thrownness), existence (projection), and falling. As Be-ing, *Da-Sein* is something that has been thrown; it has been brought into its 'there,' but *not* of its own accord." (1962: 329, H. 284). This is tantamount to saying that we are continually placed into situations we did not authentically choose, until we are brought face to face with our self be-ing t/here, from t/here we can take hold of our future thrownness.

Thus, we have seen how authenticity relates to the most primordial of the constitutive principles in Heidegger, we can now see how the remaining two principles of actualization relate.

For Heidegger, "resoluteness" functions as a condition for the possibility of integrity and sincerity. Here we can witness its relation to conscience.

> The disclosedness of *Da-Sein* [be-ing t/here] in wanting to have a conscience, is thus constituted by anxiety as attunement, by understanding as a projection of oneself upon one's ownmost Be-ing-guilty, and by discourse

> as reticence. This distinctive and authentic disclosedness, which is attested in *Da-Sein* [be-ing t/here] itself by its conscience – *this reticent self-projection upon one's ownmost Be-ing-guilty, in which one is ready for anxiety* – we call *"resoluteness."* (1962: 343, H. 296-7).

Resoluteness, like the term for "making a New Year's resolution,"[28] speaks to taking a stand in regard to the future.

> In resoluteness we have now arrived at the truth of *Da-Sein* [be-ing t/here] which is most primordial because it is authentic. Whenever a 'there' is disclosed, its whole Be-ing-in-the-world – that is to say, the world, Being-in, and the Self which, as an 'I am,' this entity is – is disclosed with equal primordiality." (Ibid).

Resoluteness is the truth of be-ing t/here, because by way of it, the existing individual can take hold of its own existence in its process of be-ing care thrown at death. It is also by way of resoluteness that an individual actualizes authenticity. In contrast to be-ing absorbed in a world, *resolution frees be-ing for its world*.

For Heidegger, resoluteness weaves through the actualization principles like mystery weaves through the constitutional ones. This can be seen in the following passages with which he linked resoluteness to Be-ing-a-whole (integrity) and authentic be-ing.

> Resoluteness, as *authentic Be-ing-one's-self*, does not detach *Da-Sein* [be-ing t/here] from its world, nor does it isolate it so that it becomes a

---

[28] Recall *Amor Fati* was Nietzsche's New Year's *resolution*.

> free-floating "I"... Resoluteness brings the self right into its current concernful Be-ing-alongside... In the light of the "for-the-sake-of-which" of one's self-chosen potentiality-for-Be-ing, resolute *Da-Sein* [be-ing t/here] frees itself for its world. (1962: 433, H. 298).

Thus, resoluteness differs from the inauthentic relation to thrownness, since "Resoluteness does not first take cognizance of a situation and put that situation before itself; it has put itself into that situation already." (1962: 347, H. 300). Resoluteness can accomplish putting itself into a future situation because it orients itself *as care* appropriately to its future. "*Resoluteness, however, is only that authenticity which, in care, is that object of care, and which is possible as care – the authenticity of care itself.*" (1962: 348, H. 301).

Hence, we can see how resoluteness, which is another word for the principle of sincerity, manifests integrity across time and the integration of the individual's mineness.

> An authentic potentiality-for-Be-ing-a-whole on the part of *Da-Sein* [be-ing t/here] has been projected existentially. By analyzing this phenomenon, we have revealed that authentic Be-ing-toward-death is anticipation. *Da-Sein*'s authentic potentiality-for-Be-ing... has been exhibited, and at the same time existentially interpreted, as resoluteness. (Ibid: 349, H. 301-2).

Clearly, the resoluteness that conditions and sustains authenticity and integrity is a movement toward mineness and away from worldliness. "Authentic Be-ing-one's-self takes the definite form of [a] ... modification of the 'they'; and this modification must be defined existentially." (1962: 312, H. 267).

Further, our priming paraphrase was also correct when in it we indicated that the entire process of care thrown at death can be articulated in terms of time. According to Heidegger, "the authenticity and inauthenticity of *Da-Sein* [be-ing t/here], are grounded ontologically on possible temporalizations of temporality." (1962: 352, H. 304). For, the resolution of resoluteness "*resolves to keep repeating itself.*" (1962: 355, H. 308). Thus, it makes sense that authentic be-ing may feel alienated from others *in the world,* since

> If with this phenomenon we have reached a way of Be-ing of *Da-Sein* [be-ing t/here] in which it brings itself to itself and face to face with itself, then this phenomenon must ... remain unintelligible to the everyday common-sense manner in which *Da-Sein* [be-ing t/here] has been interpreted by the "they." (1962: 357, H. 310).

Moreover, though authentic *Da-Sein* resolves to keep repeating itself, its experience of this repetition is as integration, continuity, and wholeness. Of course, it is in the throw of Be-ing-toward-death that all of this comes to light.

For Heidegger, as with all existentialists, the relation to death is potentially revelatory. "*Da-Sein* [be-ing t/here] is constituted by disclosedness – that is, by an understanding with an attunement. *Authentic* Be-ing-toward-death can *not evade* its ownmost non-relational possibility, or *cover up* this possibility by thus fleeing" (1962: 304, H. 260). Therefore,

> The existential conception of death has been established; and therewith we have also established what it is that an authentic Be-ing-toward-the-end should be able to comport itself

> toward. We have also characterized inauthentic Be-ing-toward-death, and thus we have prescribed in a negative way how it is possible for authentic Be-ing-toward-death *not* to be. It is with these positive and prohibitive instructions that the existential edifice of an authentic Be-ing-toward-death must let itself be projected. (Ibid).

For, death is, as Kierkegaard, Nietzsche, and Sartre all agree, inevitable for us mortals; an insight expressed well by the following celebrated turn of phrase from Ernest Hemingway (1899-1961).

> The world breaks everyone and afterward many are strong at the broken places. But those who will not break, it kills. It kills the very good and the very gentle and the very brave impartially. If you are none of these, you can be sure it will kill you too... (Hemingway, 2014: 216).

I especially like this quote in relation to existentialism because he framed the inevitableness of death in terms of the world. Death is *always* already our ownmost potential.

Finally, rounding out our discussion of the principles of existentialism instantiated in Heidegger's *Being & Time*,

> Be-ing-toward-death is the anticipation of a potentiality-for-Be-ing of that entity whose kind of Be-ing is anticipation itself. In the anticipatory revealing of this potentiality-for-Be-ing, *Da-Sein* [be-ing t/here] discloses itself to itself as regards its uttermost possibility... Anticipation turns out to be the possibility of understanding one's ownmost and uttermost

The "Philosophical Genealogy" Answer

> potentiality-for-Be-ing – that is to say, the possibility of authentic existence. (1962: 307, H. 262-3).

Having taken hold of our potentiality by taking hold of our thrownness, we actualize the freedom of the authentic be-ing of our mineness as care and resolve to repeat ourselves as authentic be-ing in the future, we anticipate how to navigate reality so as to resist falling (back) into the world.

§6 Sartre, *Being & Nothingness*: Apparitional Consciousness, Existential Meaninglessness, and *from* Willing as Valuating *to* Responsibility to Subjectivity

Jean-Paul Sartre (1905-1980) has been – mistakenly – considered the quintessential existentialist for some time now. In fact, many philosophers and professors have, unfortunately, taken to considering Sartre's articulation of existential philosophy the standard. Thus, for many, Sartre's philosophy is considered the answer to the question, "What is existentialism?" However, though I do consider Sartre's philosophy a kind of existentialism, I do *not* consider any phase of his philosophy to be the origin or the best example of existentialism.

This section is divided into the following sub-sections: {1} the phases of Sartre's philosophizing; {2} a statement of the Cartesianisms and Hegelianisms which plague the constitutional principles of Sartre's existential philosophy; {3} Sartre's characterization of "the For-itself" as an apparitional consciousness constituting the existing subject; {4} Sartre's characterization of the For-itself in regard to time and his affirmation of Descartes' *cogito ergo sum*; {5} Sartre's "trinity of lack"; {6} Sartre's characterization of the actualization principles of existentialism.

{1} Sartre's point of view regarding philosophy and his approach to philosophy changed over the years. Here is the list, endorsed by Sartre scholars, of the standard four phases of Sartre's philosophy: (1) phenomenology, (2) existentialism, (3) Marxism; (4) philosophical biography (cf. Aronson, 1980). This historical insight is helpful for recognizing that in phase one Sartre was Husserlian, and, thereby, imported Edmund Husserl's Cartesian understanding of subjectivity and preoccupation with consciousness. Thus, in phase two, Sartre's existentialism is an amalgamation of Husserl's phenomenology and Heidegger's "existential analysis" from *Being & Time*.

{2} As a result, Sartre's existentialism misunderstood what we, in this book, have called the constitutional principles of existentialism, because he remained too Cartesian in his ontology. However, with his characterization of what we call the actualization principles, Sartre infamously adopted the point of view – albeit perverted and masked – of Kantian ethics (cf. Herbert, 2016). Hence, Sartre's existential philosophy is actually the anomaly, not the exemplar, among the existential philosophies of Kierkegaard, Nietzsche, and Heidegger.

We will not overly dwell on the Cartesianism of Sartre in this section any more than we must.[29] Rather, Sartre's existential philosophy will be presented here in an essentially non-critical way. Sartre's existential philosophy receives such sufficient critique throughout the rest of this two-volume set, that I thought it was only fair to him to attempt to show his philosophy charitably, and "in the best light" in the section of this chapter devoted to it.

---

[29] It's worth noting that this discussion in Sartre directly relates to §4 of Ch.1 above, that is, the transcendental unity of apperception.

The "Philosophical Genealogy" Answer

{3} Ultimately, the remainder of this section is devoted to providing an articulation of Sartre's philosophy in regard to the seven principles of existentialism; however, the complicated nature of Sartre's ontology calls for multiple steps in this process. For example, because Sartre's characterization of the first principle – mystery – is plagued by explicit Cartesian- and Hegelian-isms (cf. Copleston, 1994), we will need to spend a number of paragraphs getting clear on what Sartre meant by his use of the terms "the In-itself" (*en-soi*) and "the For-itself" (*pour-soi*) from (what, at least, for our purpose is) his best work, *Being & Nothingness* (1943).[30]

This distinction is directly analogous to what we call the distinction between be-ing and consciousness. Recall that mystery comes from the manner in which reality and existence exceed consciousness: since consciousness is merely a part of, and an expression of, be-ing, it is incapable of comprehending the totality of universal Be-ing. However, that is *not* Sartre's understanding.

Rather, he preferred to treat the distinction as indicating aspects of a whole, that is, a whole consciousness or "consciousness only" kind of theory. Opting not to embrace the transcendental characterization of reality as exceeding consciousness, Sartre takes the Cartesian approach of considering the distinction between mind and reality to be internal to the *mind* thinking it; hence, consciousness only.

In many places and in many ways, I have argued against this Cartesian ontology in favor of Kant's transcendental ontology. Yet, to be as charitable as possible to Sartre, we will

---

[30] Toward being transparently charitable to Sartre, the following discussion of his existential philosophy will be guided by secondary sources, written by Sartre scholars, translators, and experts.

present his argument guided by Desan's "structures" of the In-itself and the For-itself. Desan began his explication of these two concepts beginning with the For-itself.

Desan reminds us that in Sartre's 1936 *The Transcendence of the Ego*, Sartre criticized Husserl stating we do not need to posit a "unifying link of our representations." (Desan, 1960: 27). Desan did an excellent job of bridging this insight to the distinction between the In-itself and the For-itself.

> This cutting down of the Ego is an essential factor in Sartre's phenomenological approach... to show that being in the full sense is objective exteriority, and that consciousness, reaching being *in itself*, reaches it as something *external*... consequently the For-itself, subjectivity, is nothing but emptiness of Being-in-itself. (Desan, 1960: 29).

Be sure to notice the description of be-ing as "*objective exteriority*." Desan clarified this by noting, "It is thus supremely important to show that the For-itself never exists *for-itself* but only for the object, and that subjectivity is a consciousness *without Subject*." (Ibid). After discussing Desan's explication of these concepts, we will consider two more commentators who have shown explicitly how this aspect of Sartre's ontology stems from his inheritance of the "Cartesian Legacy."

Because Sartre has such a conception of the ground of be-ing, it followed for him that "all operations, intentional or psychological or other, are in one way or another 'nihilations.'" (Ibid). Thus,

> Once the ensemble of structures of the For-itself has been inventoried, and once it has appeared that they are made out of nothingness, Sartre

> can claim that all their substantial value is borrowed from the outside: from the being which they *point at*. One ought thus to expel from consciousness all that could give it consistency. (Desan, 1960: 29).

The lack of "consistency" associated with a consciousness whose structures are made of nothingness, confirms the constitution of consciousness in Sartre's ontology as "apparitional." } ?

Thus, the nihilations that constitute the structures of the For-itself, are: non-personal, non-substantial, "lack and desire, and the For-itself as haunted by values and possibles." (Desan, 1960: xi). As Sartre himself put it, "Yet the For-itself *is*. It *is*, we may say, even if it is a being which is not what it is and which is what it is not." (Sartre, 1992: 79). Thus, ontologically and constitutionally speaking, Sartre's characterization of the For-itself is – contrary to especially Kant, Kierkegaard, and Nietzsche – not *personal*.

Further, the non-substantiality aspect of Sartre's structure is described – rightly – by Desan as Descartes' *cogito* stripped of substantiality.

> We ought, then, in Sartre's view, to start from the pre-reflexive *cogito*, i.e. from the consciousness which is the consciousness of something. This is intentionality. And if for a moment we should try to give consciousness a kind of being which would belong to itself alone, we should have a form of nothingness (Desan, 1960: 30).

Hazel Barnes' (1915-2008) characterization of this insight from her Translator's Introduction to *Being & Nothingness* provides further clarification regarding Sartre's ontology of the *cogito*. "It is not a merging with a higher power but a realization of one's isolation, not a vision of eternity but the perception that one is wholly process, the making of a Self with which one cannot be united." (Barnes, 1992: xxxi).

{4} Further, we need to take this *static* conception from Barnes and Desan, and understand it dynamically in terms of Sartre's three ec-*stases*.

> [1] In the present the For-itself *is* not anything. But it *is* present to the In-itself. In the light of what the For-itself chooses to make of the past (by which is meant that which the For-itself has been, an in-itself from which it is now separated by a nothingness) the For-itself thrusts itself toward the Future by choosing the Self which it will be. (2) The reflection by which the For-itself reflects on its original nihilation (a process known as pure reflection) and on its psychic states (impure reflection). (3) Being-for-others when the For-itself realizes that it has a Self which exists for the Other and which it can never know. (Barnes, 1992: xl).

Despite these three ways in which the For-itself stands-out *from itself*, it remains – for Sartre – ultimately nothing. This "wholly process" can be seen, perhaps most clearly, from the first of the three ways noted by Barnes. Consciousness arises in such a way that it selectively attaches to its past by (ontologically) selective memory and its future by way of projecting itself. Yet, these internal negations of itself reveal its "inconsistency."

Whereas Barnes noted, "the For-itself thrusts itself toward the Future by choosing the Self which it will be" (Ibid), for Desan the "Future is, above all, a relation and a position of

Self to *Self* (of For-itself to For-itself)." (1960: 39). This is how we can understand that, for Sartre, instead of be-ing, we "have to be." For, we find ourselves in that process which Barnes called "the making of a Self with which one cannot be united." Yet, in facing the future, the For-itself cannot escape this *process*.

In other words, "It is the For-itself that *posits itself*" and when the For-itself posits itself, it posits itself *"as not being the In-itself."* (Desan, 1960: 31). For Sartre, then, the reason the For-itself cannot escape this process is because, ontologically, the For-itself is characterized "as lack and desire." Thus, we need to consider lack and desire, if we are to understand the ontology of the constitutional principles of Sartre's existential philosophy.

In a section titled "The Facticity of the For-itself," Sartre entered into a discussion of Descartes, explicitly returning to Descartes' *cogito ergo sum*, and – despite Heidegger's "destruction" of this Cartesianism, Sartre takes it as a point of departure. According to Sartre,

> When Descartes wants to profit from this revelation, he apprehends himself as an imperfect being "since he doubts." But in this imperfect being, he establishes the presence of the idea of perfection. He apprehends then a cleavage between the type of being which he can conceive and the being which he is. It is this cleavage or lack of being which is at the origin of the second proof of the existence of God. (1992: 79-80). [31]

---

[31] I must comment on this. First, notice that Sartre admits that the complete or "perfect" type of being under consideration by Descartes is God. However, Sartre immediately calls that type of being the individual who is doubting. So, on the one hand, we can see the foreshadowing of

In the next section, then of *Being & Nothingness* titled "Immediate Structure of the For-Itself," Sartre explicitly draws this Cartesian conclusion, noting "The existence of desire as a human fact is sufficient to prove that human reality is a lack." (1992: 82).

Desan's characterization is helpful here because it seeks to paraphrase multiple insights in Sartre.

> The fact that the For-itself is a lack appears still more clearly in Sartre's consideration of desire. "Desire is a lack of being." All lack now is lack of being... All that lacks is lacking in ... for ... [ellipses in the original]. The For-itself is *constituted* [emphasis added] through the negation of a certain thing in order to be a certain way... Thus, by nature, the *cogito* (or consciousness in its pre-reflexive form) points to what it lacks... (1960: 32).

For, rather than characterize the existing individual as individualized transcendental be-ing, for Sartre the individual is characterized by a lack of being. Moreover, Sartre was not building off the nihilations internal to thrownness and

---

a move that Sartre will need to make in order for his existential philosophy to be coherent, and that is his silly insistence that "man wants to be God." This statement is silly for a number of reasons, not the least of which is that Sartre supposedly doesn't even believe God exists. Second, as I will discuss by commenting back in the text, Sartre reveals here that he has not only taken Descartes' *cogito* as his point of departure, but also that he has reverse engineered Descartes' "second argument for the existence of God" to ground his ontology of lack. Anyone truly familiar with the history of philosophy will understand that Sartre's strategy for constructing a constitutive ontology of the existing individual by way of "updating" Descartes was doomed from the beginning – Descartes did not think into the transcendental dimension.

The "Philosophical Genealogy" Answer

projection in Heidegger's *Being & Time*; rather, the For-itself is itself constituted by nihilations. This is an explicit denial of Kant's Transcendental Unity of Apperception.[32]

In regard to lack, we have yet to get clear on how Sartre understood the In-Itself. Sartre provided excellent clarity on this topic while discussing "the trinity of lack." According to Sartre,

> Of all internal negations, the one which penetrates most deeply into being, the one which constitutes *in its being* the being concerning which it makes the denial along with the being which it denies – this negation is *lack. This lack does not belong to the nature of the In-itself* [emphasis added], which is all positivity. [Lack] appears in the world only with the upsurge of human reality. It is only in the human *world* [emphasis added] that there can be lacks. (1992: 135).

On the one hand, the first sentence in this passage corresponds directly with Desan's clarification, above, "It is the For-itself that *posits itself*" and when the For-itself posits itself, it posits itself "*as not being the In-itself*." (1960: 31). Thus, the internal negation known as lack is the For-itself positing itself as not the In-itself.

On the other hand, consider the two places in the passage with added emphasis. First, it is important to remember that lack belongs to the For-itself, not the In-itself. Second, notice that worldliness in Sartre will be negative, just like

---

[32] For Schopenhauer – who in many ways may be understood as more pessimistic than Sartre – desire is a central human fact, but it is not a "lack." Thus, the modality of Sartre's conclusion is incorrect, the fact of human reality need not *necessarily* be "a lack."

mineness; however, the negativity of mineness is more primordial than the negativity of the world insofar as for the world to have meaning it must be thematically built up from the lack that belongs to the For-itself as mineness.

{5} Immediately following Sartre's passage above we find announced the trinity of lack. "A lack presupposes a trinity." (1992: 135).

> [1] that which is missing or "the lacking," [2] that which misses what is lacking or "the existing," and [3] a totality which has been broken by the lacking and which would be restored by the synthesis of "the lacking" and "the existing" – this is "the lacked." (Ibid).

Thus, the trinity of lack is composed of "the lacking," "the existing," and "the lacked." Here is the concrete example Sartre provided toward clarification by analogy:

> For example, if I say that the moon is not full and that one quarter is lacking, I base this judgment on full intuition of the crescent moon. Thus, what is released to intuition is *an In-itself which by itself is neither complete nor incomplete but which simply is what it is* [emphasis added], without relation to other beings. (Sartre, 1992: 135).

Before concluding the thought about the crescent moon, notice regarding the emphasis that it shows how to understand the In-itself in regard to lack, namely, the In-itself is *not lacking*.

Picking back up with the concrete example of the crescent moon, Sartre makes the analogy explicit.

> In order for this In-itself to be grasped as the crescent moon [that is, as *lacking*], it is

> necessary that a human reality surpass the given [that is, the *existing*] toward the project of the realized totality – here the disk of the full moon [that is, the *lacked*] – and return toward the given to constitute it as the crescent moon; that is, in order to realize it in its being in terms of the totality which becomes its foundation... It is the full moon which confers on the crescent moon its being as crescent; what-is-not determines what-is. (1992: 135-6).

Beginning with the last sentence, the For-itself determines the meaning of the In-itself, and it does so as a nihilation, that is, through a process of internal negation through which a given Thing becomes "grasped *as*" an object. In other words, were there no human reality, the "given" that is understood by the For-itself as the crescent moon would simply be an unknown Thing-In-itself.

The objectivation process is such that when we encounter a Thing, we experience and understand it *as* an object. Thus, the classical philosophical problem of the difference between the Thing and the object-of-experience is operable here for Sartre. Moreover, Sartre is exploiting Kant's understanding of the Thing-*in*-Itself[33] by suggesting that the Thing does not have meaning until humans confer meaning on it, and, of course, this is where the trinity of lack comes in, for Sartre, to account for the meaning-making process.[34] "It is in

---

[33] The difference between "Thing-*In*-itself" and "Thing-*in*-Itself" is intentional on my part to point to Sartre and Kant, respectively.

[34] It's worth pointing out here that Sartre could have followed all the other existentialists discussed here by considering the In-itself mysterious, that is, in terms of the principle of mystery. However, Sartre

the being of the existing, as the correlate of a human transcendence, to lead outside itself to the being which it is not – as to its meaning." (Sartre, 1992: 136). In this way, outside the For-itself's negation of itself to make itself meaningful, there is the nothingness of the Thing-*In*-Itself.

Notice that – though Sartre is not announcing his moves as he goes – he is clearly working with the "as structure," "Being-a-whole," and "projection" onto a "potentiality-for-being" in Heidegger (cf. 1962: 425, H. 373). In light of Heidegger, here, we may say that by making the connectedness of the existing individual's For-itself in one moment with a For-itself in another moment the condition for the existing individual's Be-ing-in-time, rather than the existing individual's Be-ing-in-time being the condition for the For-itself, Be-ing seemed to Sartre to be Nothing. Not even a mystery.

Before moving on to consider Sartre's principles of actualization, it is absolutely worth considering one of his paraphrasing characterizations of the sum of this "wholly process,"

> this apprehension of being as a lack of being in the face of being is first a comprehension on the part of the *cogito* of its own contingency. *I think, therefore I am* [emphasis added]. What am I? A being which is not its own foundation... (Ibid: 80).

Sartre's conclusion here plays as a double entendre. First, the lacking For-itself constitutes itself in terms of the existing as its foundation, which it *is not*. Second, the For-itself constitutes

---

seemed to think that the application of neither/nor logic seems to determine the meaning of the In-itself *as it is in itself*. Yet, with all due respect, that is an onto-logical mistake.

The "Philosophical Genealogy" Answer

itself in terms of the lacked as its foundation, though the lacked is also non-existing; it is a foundation of negation. And, as founded by and through a process of negation, it is, ultimately, wholly (negative) process.

{6} Okay, what has been said so far in this section sufficiently characterizes the constitutional principles of Sartre's ontology: (i) Nothingness, not mystery, (ii) selective recollection and choice as ontologically free and constitutive of meaning-making, and (iii) inconsistency, that is, the supposed consistency of mineness as merely the consistency of a process of negation,[35] (iv) of course, this abysmal freedom dizzies be-ing with anxiety. So, we are now in a position to discuss his expression of the principles of actualization.

That is to say, Sartre valued integrity, and integrity pertains to Be-ing-in-time authentically and with wholeness. So, even though Sartre's characterization of the ontology of authenticity, wholeness, and Be-ing-in-time are anomalous in regard to the framework of existentialism, his philosophy counts as an existentialism in that (1) existentialism is an "ethics as first philosophy" philosophy, and (2) the value of his understanding of authenticity and integrity can eclipse his ontology and make the philosophy of his second phase, ultimately, an existentialism. Yet, lastly, Sartre's understanding of meaning-making in terms of lack positioned him in such a

---

[35] Notice that, in technical terms, Sartre has confused an ontological-existential element with an existentiell element. My wanting to stand on the chair to reach an item on a shelf changes neither the meaning nor the be-ing of the chair, and if I can't reach the item, it doesn't mean the chair is lacking; for – in terms of an accurate ontology of reality – for a chair to be *actually* lacking it would need to be lacking in its chairness, but insofar as it is a chair, it is not *actually* lacking. Sartre has conflated whatness and purpose.

way that he was unable to recognize the value of sincerity, that is, the third of the three principles of actualization.[36]

It is due to the peculiarity of Sartre's meaning-making process, then, that the explication of the final part of the structure of the For-itself – the ontology of desire – belongs in the context of the actualization principles.

In this way, Desan's discussion of Sartre's development of the "lacking" and the "lacked" can provide us with further clarity: "We can give a specific name to this being which the For-itself continually desires. It is 'value.'" (1960: 34). As Desan put it, "Sartre is here completely relativistic: I am the being by which the values exist"; for, "Value is one of those notions which *enter into reality* [emphasis added] through the apparition of human consciousness. Value reveals itself through a human being who considers this or that as a value and gives it, *ipso facto*, its existence." (Ibid). In other words, just as the lacking makes *meaning* in regard to the existing by way of the lacked, so too, we desire something that we have made *meaningful* as valuable. Hence, the For-itself determines the meaning of something as desirable by way of an internal negation of the For-itself, and by way of conflation: what is desired is determined and understood by what is lacked by the For-itself.

Doubly helpful for us, the commentaries of Debra Bergoffen and Dorothy Leland provide clarification of the final part of the structure of the For-itself – the ontology of desire – as it relates to the "Cartesian Legacy" and Husserl's phenomenology. According to Bergoffen,

---

[36] Sartre's misunderstanding of sincerity is so striking that it merely calls for a footnote to illustrate: Sartre failed to see that when one is be-ing ironic, one is be-ing *sincerely* ironic. Moreover, one cannot be ironically sincere. It only works in the former direction.

The "Philosophical Genealogy" Answer

> *There is no transcendental point of reference* [emphasis added]. I am always and only an embodied subject. The idea that the self is a soul/mind distinct from the body is not, however, the whole of Descartes' thesis of the self. There is another component of his theory of subjectivity: the idea that the body is a source of alienation. Descartes' thesis is not simply that the body is not the self, but more complexly that the body claims to be the self and that we are lured by this claim away from ourselves. It is from this more complex claim that the echoes of Descartes find a place in Sartre's thought. (Bergoffen, 1992: 235).

One way to paraphrase Bergoffen's brilliant insight here is by way of analogy. Thus, the body for Descartes *analogously* translates into Sartre's ontology as the In-itself, and the mind in Descartes *analogously* translates into the For-itself as apparitional consciousness. Further, then, given Desan's excellent explication of the In-itself and For-itself above, it is clear that Sartre updated the Cartesian play of alienation through his engagement with Husserl.

On the one hand, Bergoffen's comments regarding this update are worth quoting at length.

> Like Descartes, Sartre recognizes the unique and intimate relationship between perception and my experience of myself as body. Because Sartre recognizes the subject as embodied, he cannot take this relationship lightly. He must undertake an extensive examination of the relationship between subjectivity and

> perceptual experience. These examinations take two directions. (Bergoffen, 1992: 235).

According to Bergoffen, these two directions are "bad faith" and "the look." For the former: "it is a question of how I use my perception of myself as body to escape my freedom/subjectivity, e.g., the woman in the café, the homosexual" and for the latter: "it is a question of how, by being an embodied subject available to the perceptions of the other, I am vulnerable to the loss and exploitation of my freedom/subjectivity." (Ibid).

Reaffirming Desan's characterization of the For-itself as an "apparitional consciousness," Bergoffen concluded her above thoughts by showing how Sartre's thinking here ties back into Descartes'.

> Where for Descartes the body alienates me from myself by substituting its otherness for my essence, *for Sartre the body's powers of alienation are grounded in its being inextricably intertwined with human subjectivity* [emphasis added]. It is because the body is not an other that the other encounters me in it. (Ibid).

Thus, Bergoffen's characterization fills in the analogy with Descartes' ontology.

On the other hand, Deborah Leland's commentary on the "Cartesian Legacy" of Sartre's ontology ties Bergoffen and Desan together well.

> Although the view of the *cogito* offered to us in *The Transcendence of the Ego* is modified somewhat in *Being and Nothingness*, we find in this early work the germination of the dualism which later plagues Sartre's ontology. (Leland, 2004: 154).

The "Philosophical Genealogy" Answer

According to Leland, "Sartre, of course, denies that consciousness is dual; yet the unity which he gives to consciousness is threatened by his insistence that consciousness possesses an 'immanent' consciousness of itself." (Ibid). Thus,

> While rejecting a dualism of substance, Sartre seems to posit a duality of object and act within consciousness. In *The Transcendence of the Ego*, Sartre accepts Husserl's notion of intentionality, which redefines the Cartesian *cogito* as *cogitatio*; yet in rejecting Husserl's explanation of self-consciousness, Sartre reintroduces Descartes' immanent consciousness (of) self in the modified form of the pre-reflective *cogito*. (Leland, 2004: 154).

Notice that Leland is actually discussing the trinity of lack here. The duality of lacking and existing (because they belong to different ontological orders) constitutes a duality that Sartre then tries to unify as "a totality," "the lacked." Further, notice how "intentionality" is positioned to constitutionally account for the "values" of integrity and authenticity.

By way of clarifying this notion of intentionality, Leland shows how the For-itself (even though it is not for-itself) can bring the values of integrity and authenticity to its situation.

> Sartre finds that Husserl's transcendental "I" would tear consciousness from itself since consciousness is an absolute limited only by itself. Consciousness as absolute means, for Sartre, that consciousness is present to itself as the pre-cognitive foundation of all that is known to the reflecting *cogito*. This leads us directly to Sartre's notion of non-positional consciousness

– consciousness of consciousness, or consciousness which is not for itself its own object. (Leland, 2004: 154).

This is especially helpful for noticing how far from Kant Sartre wandered in that Sartre denies the transcendental unity of apperception as the transcendental be-ing of the existing individual In-itself. Rather, caught in its own process of negation, apparitionally manifesting through dynamics characterized in terms of a trinity of lack, Sartre considers one moment of consciousness linked to its contiguous moment of consciousness because they are both instances of consciousness.

On the one hand, this is how Sartre's ontology can suggest that "subjectivity is a consciousness *without Subject*," and that the, "For-itself never exists *for-itself* but only for the object" (Desan, 1960: 29). On the other hand, this is how the existing individual brings the values of integrity and authenticity into existence. That is to say, in the face of all this nothingness, the existing individual is inescapably caught in a looping trinity of negative freedom. It "has to be" itself, though it cannot be itself because it is not for-itself.

Through an experiential encounter with the given, the For-itself manifests to determine and understand the object of experience. Because this manifestation is constituted by an internal negation, there is no subject to which to attribute the determining and understanding of the experience. Recall, Merleau-Ponty's criticism of Sartre's ontology: It entails an understanding of consciousness as "self-referential." (Leland, 2004: 164; cf. Scalambrino, 2020a).

Thus, in the face of the existing as nothingness, the *mineness* of consciousness as the For-itself is responsible for determining and understanding the meaning of its situations in

The "Philosophical Genealogy" Answer

terms of *worldliness*. Just as with other existentialists, then, Sartre was up against the principle of sincerity as the principle of the connection between mineness and worldliness; however, he outright denied it (cf. 1992: 100-105). That is, Sartre set sincerity up as a (strawman) principle of be-ing, then rejected it as exemplary of bad faith; yet, sincerity is a principle of action *in regard to situations*.

The triad involved is sincerity, irony, coherency. So long as action is coherent, then it is either sincerely sincere or sincerely ironic. There is no ironic sincerity without being incoherent. Therefore, in the order of coherent action, sincerity is more primordial than irony. It is only in relation to the ontology of the Thing-*in*-Itself beyond our capacity to *coherently* experience it that irony becomes more primordial, since the Thing is not experienced as it is in-itself.

Returning to the principles of actualization, then, it is sincere action in the face of the nothingness of existential meaninglessness that acknowledges the nothingness of apparitional consciousness and resolutely "seeks to flee the inner dis[-]integration of ... being in the direction of the In-itself, which it should be and is not." (Sartre, 1992: 116). Despite there being no subject, the apparitional consciousness of the For-itself as the embodied subject remains in good faith (that is, an authentic mode) by resisting dis-integrity. To sincerely exist as the self that one has to, but cannot, be [*Being & Nothingness*], is to exist coherently with integrity and authenticity.

Finally, there is no exit from the negative process of the For-itself, which the existing individual "has to be." The dreadful ontological freedom of the negative process in the face of nothingness is inescapable. Thus, anguish (dread or anxiety) becomes the motor force for the – sincere – modality of action in the face of nothingness that allows for integrity and authenticity; that is to say, existing with integrity and authenticity despite the nothingness of worldliness and mineness is the highest actualization of the existing individual possible in the despair of Sartre's existential meaninglessness.

૭

§7 Marcel, *The Mystery of Being:* The Generative Power of Commitment, Authenticity as Participation in a Spiritual Community, and Life as Creative Sacrifice

This section is divided into the following sub-sections: {1} the phases of Gabriel Marcel's (1889-1973) philosophizing; {2} the writings examined in this section and Marcel's idea of participation; {3} worldliness, despair, and hope, regarding the existential elements of wholeness and totality; {4} how Marcel's "trinity of fidelity" culminates in creative sacrifice; {5} freedom and the spirit world; {6} Marcel's characterization of the actualization principles of existentialism.

{1} It is possible to identify three "phases" across the history of Marcel's philosophizing. These phases derive from his own reflections on the progression of his philosophizing and his choices regarding what to emphasize. These phases may be labelled (1) the metaphysical, (2) the Christian existential,[37] and (3) the personal.

---

[37] It was early in his philosophical vocation when Marcel converted to Catholicism and was baptized in 1929.

The "Philosophical Genealogy" Answer

Yet, mapping these phases to years or writings is not possible; for the content of these phases is interrelated and woven together (rhizomatic even), rather than each subsequent phase replacing the former. In fact, some commentators suggest that Marcel's philosophy never truly changed phases; they see these phases as moments, emphasizing the metaphysical, the existential, and the personal (cf. Marcel, 2009: 39).

{2} For the purpose of presenting Marcel's version of existentialism, we focus on three of his writings which were publicly presented: *The Mystery of Being*, made from his "Gifford Lectures" (1949-1950) presented at the University of Aberdeen; *The Existential Background of Human Dignity*, made from his "William James Lectures" (1961-1962) presented at Harvard University; and, his "Some Reflections on Existentialism" (1964) presented at De Paul University. In addition to these public presentations, we will consider Marcel's *Being and Having*, originally published in 1949, his *Creative Fidelity*, originally published in 1964, and two of his earlier essays: "On the Ontological Mystery" and "Existence and Human Freedom."

Now, as we will see, when Marcel begins with mystery, he immediately links it with the principle of mineness by way of the spectrum between worldliness and mineness; however, this may be difficult to notice, at first, because, for example, "to enter into the depths of one's self means here to fundamentally get outside of one's self." (1950: 131). The quickest way to understand this is by way of how Marcel essentially distanced himself from the Cartesian Legacy haunting French philosophy.

To use Marcel's own way of characterizing the difference, whereas Descartes' approach to the subject was indicative of a "spectator" view, Marcel endorsed, in contrast, a "participatory" or "participant" view of mineness. It is in this way that Marcel can, **on the one hand**, relate to worldliness like all the other existentialists; he even referred to it as "broken." Rather than be absorbed in the world, inauthentic individuals participate in a broken world. Thus, he characterized worldliness as "functionalized," "problematized," and "empty," and mineness as "faithful," "mysterious," and "full." This is despair, slave mentality, inauthenticity, and bad faith in the vocabularies of Kierkegaard, Nietzsche, Heidegger, and Sartre, respectively.

On the other hand, because Marcel understood mineness as participatory, he understood self-actualization as participation – not in worldliness, but – in a higher, spiritual, community. Thus, self-actualization allows one to "get outside of one's self" in that through it one enters into communion with – what in this book we have referred to as – transcendental be-ing. With all others participating in his higher communion, the authentically-existing individual has entered into participation in a spiritual community. Of course, this is not like having a magazine subscription; rather, according to Marcel, this is a genuine fellowship through participation in the presence of transcendental be-ing (cf. Willcutt, 2020).

{3} In his "On the Ontological Mystery," Marcel explained that "To raise the ontological problem is to raise the question of being as a whole and of oneself seen as a totality." (2002: 17). This language of "being as a whole" and "oneself seen as a totality" should remind us of Heidegger's *Being & Time*. This should also remind us of Kierkegaard's antidote to despair, that is: be-ing one self and be-ing one's self. This is also the point of the thought exercise Nietzsche called the idea of the Eternal Recurrence of the Same; a thought exercise that he

The "Philosophical Genealogy" Answer

believed should end in *amor fati*. And, in terms of the principles of existentialism, these two "questions" brought forth by "raising" the ontological problem are integrity and sincerity.

Further, we may organize Marcel's terminology according to terms for the inauthentic and authentic modes of mineness. While the former, for Marcel, refers to a nihilistic world of despair, the latter refers to fidelity and hope. Similarly, Marcel often used the juxtaposition of two analogous series of terms to articulate his existential philosophy.

> Hence, between hope – the reality of hope in the heart of the one whom it inhabits – and the judgment brought to bear upon it by a mind chained to objectivity, there exists the same barrier as that which separates a pure mystery from a pure problem. (Marcel, 2002: 30).

Hope versus objective inference coincides with mystery and problem, respectively. And, in this way, hope and awareness of mystery regarding existence belong with authenticity as fruits of existential actualization.

Marcel clarified and extended the series associated with despair in terms of functionality, fear, and desire.

> The world of the problematical is the world of fear and desire, which are inseparable; at the same time, it is that world of the functional... finally, it is the kingdom of technics of whatever sort. Every technique serves, or can be made to serve, some desire or some fear; conversely every desire as every fear tends to invent its appropriate technique. (2002: 30).

Though Marcel didn't use the idea of death to clarify his position in this passage, bringing it into the conversation here helps.

Thus, despair and nihilistic understandings of Be-ing-in-the-world – Hegel's nihilisms of Be-ing-as-History and Be-ing-as-Speculative-System – determine the meaning of, and understand, death as merely no longer Be-ing-in-the-world.

Just as it is despair to understand the meaning of life as the attempt to be-in-the-world as long as possible, so too it is inauthentic to want to be-in-the-world forever (cf. Marcel, 1963: 141). Whereas it is an empirical critique to say that such a person may be pathetic, it is an ontological critique to say they are being inauthentic. According to Marcel, a person in despair understands as bad the fact that we do not have technology with which to extend life indefinitely: "From this standpoint, despair consists in the recognition of the ultimate inefficacy of all technics" (2002: 30). Despair sees mineness in terms of functionality and worldliness in terms of problems. For, "we seem nowadays to have entered upon the very era of despair; we have not ceased to believe in technics, that is to envisage reality as a complex of problems..." (Ibid).

To combat this, Marcel invokes his existential idea of fidelity. It is in his attempt to clarify this idea that his discussion of mineness and death are especially helpful. Though fidelity may be elucidated regarding either the inauthentic or authentic standpoints, when it is understood from the authentic standpoint it shows how Marcel envisioned hope in contrast to despair. "Fidelity to a principle as a principle is idolatry in the etymological sense of the word... So little is [authentic] fidelity akin to the inertia of conformism that it implies an active and continuous struggle..." (2002: 35). And, how one falls into despair is stated regarding mineness.

The question of "Who am I?" appears in all existential philosophies. Thus, Marcel's way of meeting this criterion: "it is

The "Philosophical Genealogy" Answer

not possible to count on a friend, a party, or a collectivity to decide [who I am] for me, [so] the question becomes an appeal ([a] call)." (1950: xii). And, following his usual formula of juxtaposition, Marcel explained that "my life" may be understood in two different ways, namely in accordance with inauthenticity or authenticity. Thus, "*My life* can be considered from two standpoints, that of: (1) The past. (2) That of the present, the fact that I am still living it." (Marcel, 1950: xii).

As we can see, Marcel's theory of temporality is easier to handle than Heidegger's. Here, Marcel associated understanding life from the standpoint of the past with an inauthentic mode of mineness and from the standpoint of the present with an authentic mode. Whereas meaning-making – especially regarding "my life" – from the standpoint of *pastness* indicates inauthenticity and despair, associated with nihilism, *presence* contains the be-ing-as-a-whole indicative of the principle of integrity, and the be-ing-toward-the-end of "oneself seen as a totality" (2002: 17), the principle of sincerity.

Marcel's way of articulating this is brilliant, and, therefore, we will quote it at length.

> My life cannot, then, be reproduced by a narrative... it [its totality] lies outside the scope of my present concrete thought and can only be recaptured as... flashes of memory.
> *Nor is my life* in the notes jotted down day by day and making up my diary... *Nor is my work* to be identified with my life... *Finally, my acts*, in as much as they are recorded in objective reality, do not tell of that within me which lies beyond them. (Marcel, 1950: xiii).

Regarding the other series in the juxtaposition, then, here is Marcel, speaking in terms of the present:

> *Insofar as I am still living it,* my life appears to me as something I can *consecrate* or *sacrifice,* and the more I feel that I am striving toward an end, or serving a cause, the more alive (living) I feel... (Marcel, 1950: xiii).

Now, "consecrate," here, means to dedicate, and, of course, dedication is a kind of resolution. Just as authentic Be-ing-toward-death, for Heidegger, involved resoluteness toward wholeness and totality, Marcel characterized authentic Be-ing-toward-death less generically and more actively as: "sacrifice." (cf. Marcel, 1950: 171).

Thus, "To give one's life is neither to part with one's self nor to do away with one's self, it is to respond to a certain call. Death can then be life, in the supreme sense." (Ibid). Moreover, in clarifying his meaning, Marcel used precisely the language we have used to characterize the existential principle of mystery.

> *My life is infinitely beyond the* consciousness *I have of it at any given moment* [emphasis added]; it is essentially unequal in itself, and transcendent of the account that I am led to keep of its elements. (Marcel, 1950: xiii).

This is the existential point of view regarding the existing individual's situation in the world. In other words, "The existential point of view about reality cannot be other than that of incarnate personality." (Marcel, 1949: 10).

Therefore, it is also clear that, for Marcel, existence exceeds consciousness, and existence is a mystery.

> Thus, one's own body is a mystery; one's sensory awareness of what lies outside oneself

is a mystery; one's relation to one's family, beloved, [and] friends is a mystery; and, the way in which all of this is horizoned by a sense of the totality is the final ontological mystery. (Wood, 2005: 14).

Just as one inauthentically relates to experience in terms of objectivity, functionality, and problems, so too Marcel characterized inauthentic consciousness as "first reflection," and this is as opposed to authentic "secondary reflection" or "re-collection" (cf. Marcel, 1950: 92-3). More than just extending Marcel's juxtaposed series of terms, this also shows how Marcel did not follow Sartre's model regarding the constitutional principles of existentialism.

{4} Notice, then, that fidelity functions precisely for Marcel as resoluteness does for Heidegger.

Presence is mystery in the exact measure in which it is presence. Now, fidelity is the active perpetuation of presence, the renewal of its benefits – of its virtue which consists in a mysterious incitement to create. Here again we may be helped by the consideration of aesthetic creativeness; for if artistic creation is conceivable, it can only be on condition that the world is present to the artist in a certain way – present to his heart and to his mind, present to his very being. (2002: 36).

Similar to Nietzsche's use of "art" to characterize the authentic mode of engagement with the world and his "from artist to work of art," Marcel's above passage speaks of a creative transformation of the world. Fidelity is the futural relation to the present that sustains authentic presence in the face of continual potential to "fall" into a problematized, "broken," world, a functionalized self, and the despair of nihilism. Further, the futural relation of fidelity culminates, for Marcel, in relation to eternity, since this mystery like "every mystery is itself a river, which flows into the Eternal, as into a sea." (1950: 219).

Marcel's way of articulating freedom in relation to mineness provides insight into his understanding of the actualization principles: authenticity, integrity, and sincerity. To characterize the following discussion of Marcel's instantiation of the principles of existentialism as responding to a question: How does Marcel connect freedom to mineness and its actualizations of authenticity, integrity, and sincerity?

It is in regard to this question that we will see the uniqueness with which Marcel instantiated the principles of existentialism. Moreover, by answering this question we come to see Marcel's unique contribution to existential thinking. On the one hand, this contribution is unique despite its striking similarities to Kierkegaard's philosophy. On the other hand, much of Marcel's work regarding "existentialism" may be understood as an attempt to articulate an existential philosophy that can be seen as unique in contrast to Sartre.

To accomplish this, we will return to the discussion of fidelity and focus on its commitment component, since commitment contributes to the formation of future situations and experiences. This is what Marcel called "creative fidelity."

Whereas Kierkegaard's characterization of commitment in the face of the absurdity of the world leads to a religious integrity and authenticity, Sartre characterized commitment in the face of the meaninglessness of existence as itself leading to an atheistic integrity and authenticity. Marcel's characterization, then, of the temporal ontology of commitment

The "Philosophical Genealogy" Answer

weighs-in against Sartre by showing us the efficacy and presence found in the metaphysics of hope, while attempting to articulate an aspect of ontology missing from the thought of Kierkegaard (cf. Marcel, 1964: 250).

When I truly commit *myself,* I change the future, and I change my way of relating to whatever will emerge from the future. Notice that this unites my past and future in a present – a present in which I will remain faithful to my commitment (cf. Marcel, 2001: 65-6; cf. Marcel, 1950: 122-4). Not only, then, does this give me grounds on which to hope. My commitment is related to an anticipation. Yes, a commitment is a resolution. Notice that this is (resolute) be-ing-toward-an-end. And, it is by way of this temporal ontology that the presence of hope – as if from beyond me – re-enters the situation in which I exist, and it enlivens me.

Further, this is how commitment, creative fidelity, and hope constellate. In other words, this is the reciprocal action of creative fidelity. First, I receive a call, impelling me to respond. Second, I commit myself, and that provides access to my be-ing-a-whole. Third, I understand the meaning of the remainder of my time as a sacrifice of myself, that is, the self I am committed to be. In Heidegger's vocabulary this is taking hold of one's ownmost potentiality for be-ing.

Notice, then, the creative sacrifice aspect of commitment indicates my be-ing-toward-an-end. In terms of mineness, this allows me to actualize integrity (wholeness-across-time), authenticity (wholeness-as totality), and sincerity (sustaining commitment to finite wholeness). Of course, sincerity functions doubly – just as hope functions for Marcel; its momentum re-enters the situation in which I exist.

Hence, to answer the question we took as our point of departure: How Marcel connects freedom to mineness and its actualizations of authenticity, integrity, and sincerity forms what we may call Marcel's "trinity of fidelity" that culminates in creative sacrifice. Marcel's actualization principles cycle through this trinity: (1) creative fidelity and creative sacrifice allow me to be who I am, (2) "to say: I am free, is to say: I am myself," and (3) "By freedom I am given back to myself" (1951: vii).

{5} Now, from the point of view of the call, Marcel's articulation of the actualization principles of existentialism, as they relate to the triad of mineness, freedom, and fidelity, is also an instantiation of the spectrum of anxiety spanning the difference between worldliness and mineness. For, just as with the other existentialists, "the need for transcendence ... is experienced above all, as a kind of dissatisfaction [with the inauthentic world]" (1950: 42). Yet, here is a uniqueness for Marcel, "The problem of freedom... can itself only be stated on a certain spiritual level... Freedom is only possible in the measure of my having within me the means by which I can transcend the [anonymous] order of the *him* [*Das Man*]." (1967: 20).

Consequently, to have what Marcel called the "means within me" refers to the manner in which self-actualization is creative (and this, of course, constitutionally includes the mysterious freedom *within* mineness). It is this mysterious freedom of mineness that allows us to participate in a dimension higher and more intimate than the anonymous worldliness, that is, be-ing carried along by the nobody. For Marcel, "this freedom is a gift; yet, it is necessary for me to accept it; the power granted me to accept *or refuse it* is not separable from this gift." (2001: 101). Uniquely, Marcel not only articulates a higher spiritual community, the presence of which acts as a bulwark against *falling* into inauthenticity and the loss of freedom; thus,

> The free act is essentially a significant act... What distinguishes the free act is that it helps to make me what I am ... whereas the contingent or insignificant act, the act which might just as well be performed by anybody, has no contribution to make to this sort of creation of myself by myself... (1951: 117).

In this way, I simultaneously actualize myself as authentic and transcend the inauthentic world (and inauthentic others) in actualizing my freedom to commit myself (and my time) or not. Thus, the philosophical-existential quest to become who you are, for Marcel, appears as a conquest to win myself back from the inauthentic world where my self is initially located and into which my self can fall.

Yet, as noted above, and in completion of the trinity's cycle, the creativity of this spiritual reality also nourishes my creativity. This is self-actualizing away from, to use Heidegger's phrases, "be-ing carried along by the nobody" and away from determining and understanding the meaning of life in terms of *Das Man* or "the They" (cf. Marcel, 1973: 225-6). Though this speaks to Marcel's articulation of anxiety as a constitutional principle; importantly, this creative resistance against anonymity is not alienation; that is to say, authenticity is not alienating for Marcel; rather, we come to see a community – dare we say "kingdom" – held in be-ing by living commitments (cf. 2010: 27). Rather than be-ing carried along, this community (of persons) is sustained by living commitments.

Thus, *contra* Sartre, meaninglessness, nihilism, and alienation are not fundamental characteristics of existence, for Marcel.

> [F]idelity, unless it is to be fruitless or, worse, reduced to mere persistency, must spring from something that is "absolutely given" to me. (I feel this is especially true in my relation to the people I love best). From the very beginning there must be a sense of stewardship: Something has been entrusted to us, so that we are not only responsible toward ourselves, but toward an active and superior principle (1949: 14).

Marcel's articulation of "what has been entrusted to us" points to his most unique and original contribution to the history of existential thought. This contribution may be understood in terms of spiritual reality and by distinguishing among worlds.

Though this contribution is unique to Marcel, it takes place in the framework of existentialism regarding what we have referred to as "the three contexts for determining and understanding the meaning of life." Regarding these three contexts of meaning-making, it is as if Marcel is suggesting – along the same lines regarding the absolute that can be found in Kierkegaard, Nietzsche, and Heidegger – that the manner in which the metaphysics of hope contributes to the process of meaning-making suggests the presence of an absolute (fourth) context to be added to the three contexts.[38]

---

[38] A note of clarification is needed here. According to Emmy van Deurzen and the *APA Dictionary of Psychology* (2021), there are three (3) "*Welt*s," or "worlds," to be identified in existential thought: the *Umwelt*, the *Mitwelt*, and the *Eigenwelt*. However, as I noted previously in this book, their characterization is incorrect (based on Heidegger's own explication, which is the authority on which van Deurzen and the APA, explicitly by way of Ludwig Binswanger [1881-1966], base their definition). That is to say, they mislabel the third *Welt*, and mislocate/fail

The "Philosophical Genealogy" Answer

In other words, in light of the presence of hope an *Eigenwelt* is revealed, beyond the *Umwelt*, *Mitwelt*, and *Selbstwelt*. Of course, the difference between the *Selbstwelt* and the *Eigenwelt* is the difference between individualized incarnate transcendental be-ing (i.e., the person) and transcendental Being (i.e., spirit). In this way, we can see that it is through fidelity to the absolute that humans encounter the presence of hope.

That is to say, through the presence of the *Eigenwelt*, inter-subjectivity (and inter-personality) "plays its part within the life of the subject, even at moments when the latter's only intercourse is with itself. In its own intrinsic structure, subjectivity is already, and in the most profound sense, genuinely inter-subjective." (Marcel, 1950: 182).

{6} In this way, Marcel provides a fresh point of view for what we might call the potential of the *Mitwelt* to actualize as a spiritual *community*.[39] For, "the more my existence takes on the character of including others, the narrower becomes the gap which separates it from being; the more, in other words, I am." (1951: 151). In this way, it is as if Marcel distinguishes his existential thought from all the previous existential thinkers

---

to see the fourth *Welt*. Thus, the proper distinction is: *Umwelt*, *Mitwelt*, *Selbstwelt*, *Eigenwelt*. (In English: the physically-surrounding environment, the social world, the personal world, and the spiritual world). Whereas the first three *Welt*s correspond directly with the structure found in Kant regarding contexts for determining and understanding the meaning of life, the fourth *Welt* is revealed, or, if you prefer, unconcealed, to the existing individual through actualizing the existential principles of actualization: authenticity, integrity, and sincerity.

[39] Though it would be beyond the scope of this section to discuss thoroughly here, this idea may be understood in terms of participation in Kant's "Kingdom of Ends." Cf. Scalambrino (2016). *Introduction to Ethics: A Primer for the Western Tradition*. Dubuque, IA: Kendall Hunt.

discussed (though I believe it is, at least, implicit in Kant, Nietzsche, and Heidegger) by distinguishing the *Mitwelt* into inauthentic and authentic. The latter, of course, being the *Mitwelt* nourished by the grace of the *Eigenwelt*.

Marcel described this – reminding us of Nietzsche – through reference to artists and love: "in the scale of sanctity and of artistic creation, where freedom glows with its fullest light, [freedom] is never autonomy. For the saint and the artist alike, auto-centricity and the self are entirely swallowed up in love." (1949: 174). This helps round-out how creative fidelity relates to love and death as creative sacrifice. For, whether it is the saint or the artist

> the person who is carrying the act out has…the feeling that through self-sacrifice he is reaching his fulfillment; given his own situation and that of everything dear to him, he realizes…he most completely is, in the act of giving his life away. (1950: 166).

Love for Marcel "truly exists only when it defies absence, when it triumphs over absence, and in particular, over that absence which we hold to be—mistakenly no doubt—absolute, and which we call death." (2001: 152).

Precisely, then, as it worked in Heidegger's *Being & Time*, Be-ing-toward-death as Be-ing-toward-the-end allows one to take hold of one's ownmost potential: "[it] is death that will open the door to all we have lived on earth." (Marcel, 2001: 173). For, death can "tear us from ourselves in order to better establish us in being." (Ibid). Just as "Presence signifies more and something other than being-there; in all strictness, it cannot be said of an object that it is present." (2010: 18), so too, "fidelity is ontological in its principle, because it prolongs presence which itself corresponds to a certain kind of hold which being has on us; because it multiplies and deepens the effect of this presence almost unfathomably in our lives." (Ibid: 90-1).

Marcel described one's self-awareness of self-actualizing in terms of recognizing one's self in the *Eigenwelt* through creative fidelity and sacrifice. He called it "an exclamatory awareness of self."

> Existence and the exclamatory awareness of existence cannot really be separated; the dissociation of the two can be carried out only at the cost of robbing the subject of our investigation of its proper nature; separated from exclamatory awareness... existence tends to be reduced to its own corpse (1950: 91).

To commit and remain faithful – through intentions of belief, hope, and love – to one's wholeness and totality is a sacrifice.

Marcel is the existential thinker with whom mystery is most associated. Not only did he affirm the transcendental dimension as mysterious, but, also, he explicitly acknowledged that reality exceeds consciousness. We saw how the other constitutional principles are tied together for Marcel. That is to say, freedom and mineness intimately and positively coincide such that: the more I am myself the more free I am, and the more free I am, the more I am myself. Like the other existentialists, this can be seen along a spectrum from worldliness to mineness. Thus, fallenness in the world takes the form of temptation to fall away from mineness and freedom.

And, to conclude, Marcel's articulation of the actualization principles was quite similar to the other existentialists; however, through his concept of presence, sustained through the virtuous intentionalities of belief, hope, and love, and actualized through the be-ing-a-whole and be-ing-toward-an-end of creative fidelity and creative sacrifice brought a unique view of spiritual reality into existential focus. For Marcel, authenticity is not merely a mode of mineness but a mode of community in an authentic "world" sustained by presence.

At the same time, the actualization principles of existentialism function here in much the same way they did for the other existentialists. The integrity of be-ing-a-whole and the authenticity of be-ing-toward-an-end are both at work in Marcel's existential philosophy, and the principle of sincerity is at work in regard to the intentionalities of belief, hope, and love that constitute the mineness in communion with the spiritual reality of transcendental be-ing.

ᛒ End of Volume I ☙

Bibliography & Further Readings

Abbagnano, Nicola. (1969). *Critical Existentialism*. N. Langiulli (Trans.). New York, NY: Anchor Books.

Aronson, Ronald. (1980). *Jean-Paul Sartre: Philosophy in the World*. London: Verso.

Barnes, Hazel E. (1992). Translator's Introduction. In *Being and Nothingness: A Phenomenological Essay on Ontology*. (ix-lii) London: Washington Square Press.

Baudrillard, Jean. (2008). *The Perfect Crime*. C. Turner (Trans.). London: Verso.

de Beauvoir, Simone. (1963). *Force of Circumstance*. R. Howard (Trans.). London: Weidenfeld and Nicolson.

_____. (1989). "Merleau-Ponty and Pseudo-Sartreanism," V. Zaytzeff (Trans.). *International Studies in Philosophy* 21: 3-48.

_____. (2015). *The Ethics of Ambiguity*. B. Frechtman (Trans.). New York, NY: Citadel Press.

Benbassat, Roi. (2012). "Kierkegaard's Relation to Kantian Ethics Reconsidered," *Kierkegaard Studies Yearbook* (1): 49-74.

Bergoffen, Debra B. (1992). "Casting Shadows: The Body in Descartes, Sartre, de Beauvoir..." *Journal of French and Francophone Philosophy* 4 (2-3): 232-243.

Binswanger, Ludwig. (1968). *Being-in-the-World: Selected Papers of Ludwig Binswanger*. J. Needleman (Trans.). New York: Harper & Row.

Blanchot, Maurice. (1995). *The Work of Fire*. C. Mandell (Trans.). Stanford, CA: Stanford University Press.

Brobjer, Thomas H. (2003). "Nietzsche's Knowledge of Kierkegaard." *Journal of the History of Philosophy* 41(2): 251-263.

Camus, Albert. (1969). *Lyrical and Critical Essays*. P. Thody (Ed.) and E.C. Kennedy (Trans.). New York, NY: Alfred A. Knopf.

_____. (1992). *The Rebel: An Essay on Man in Revolt*. H. Read (Trans.). New York, NY: Alfred A. Knopf.

Carr, David. (1995). "The Question of the Subject: Heidegger and the Transcendental Tradition." *Human Studies*, 17(4): 403-418.

Compton, John J. (1997). Existential Phenomenology. In L. Embree, et al. (Eds.). *Encyclopedia of Phenomenology*. (205-208). New York: Springer.

Confucius. (1893). *The Doctrine of the Mean*. In J. Legge (Ed. & Trans.). *The Chinese Classics*. Oxford, UK: Clarendon Press.

Cooper, David E. (1999). *Existentialism: A Reconstruction*. Hoboken, NJ: Blackwell, 1999.

Copleston, Frederick. (1994). *A History of Philosophy, Volume IV*. New York, NY: Doublday.

Bibliography & Further Readings

Crowell, Steven. (2012). Existentialism and its legacy. *The Cambridge Companion to Existentialism*. (pp. 3-26). Cambridge, England: Cambridge University Press.

Deleuze, Gilles. (1994). *Difference & Repetition*. P. Patton (Trans.). New York: Columbia University.

_____. (2006). *Nietzsche and Philosophy*. H. Tomlinson (Trans.). New York: Columbia University.

Desan, Wilfrid. (1960). *The Tragic Finale: An Essay on the Philosophy of Jean-Paul Sartre*. New York, NY: Harper.

Distaso, Leonardo V. (2004). *The Paradox of Existence: Philosophy and aesthetics in the Young Schelling*. Dordrecht, The Netherlands: Kluwer Academic Publishers.

Dostoyevsky, Fyodor. (1928). *The Gambler*, in *The Novels of Fyodor Dostoevsky*, Vol. 9. London: Macmillan.

Fackenheim, Emil L. (1954). "Schelling's Conception of Positive Philosophy," *The Review of Metaphysics* 7(4): 563-582.

Fendt, Gene. (1990). *For What May I Hope? Thinking with Kant and Kierkegaard*. New York: Peter Lang.

Fischer, Roland. (1971). A Cartography of the Ecstatic and Meditative States. *Science*, New Series, 174(4012): 897-904.

Flam, Leopold. (1963). "Schelling's Romantic Dialectic." *Philosophy Today* 7: 298-308.

Flynn, Thomas R. (2006). *Existentialism: A Very Short Introduction*. Oxford, England: Oxford University Press.

Frank, Manfred. (2004). *The Philosophical Foundations of Early German Romanticism*. Albany, NY: SUNY Press.

Fulton, Ann. (1999). *Apostles of Sartre: Existentialism in America, 1945-1963*. Evanston, IL: Northwestern University Press.

Green, Ronald M. (1992). *Kierkegaard and Kant: The Hidden Debt*. Albany, NY: SUNY Press.

Grene, Marjorie. (1952). "Authenticity: An Existential Virtue," *Ethics* 62(4): 266-274.

Hart, James G. (2009). *Who One Is: Book 2 (Existenz and Transcendental Phenomenology)*. New York: Springer.

Hegel, G.W.F. (1977). *Phenomenology of Spirit*. A.V. Miller (Trans.). Oxford, England: Oxford University Press.

Hemingway, Ernest. (2014). *A Farewell to Arms*. New York, NY: Simon & Schuster.

Henrich, Dieter. (2003). *Between Kant and Hegel: Lectures on German Idealism*. Cambridge, MA: Harvard University Press.

Heidegger, Martin. (1962). *Being & Time*. J. Macquarrie and E. Robinson (Trans.). New York: Harper & Row.

_____. (1985). *A History of the Concept of Time*. T. Kisiel (Trans.). Bloomington, IN: Indiana University Press.

_____. (1988). *The Basic Problems of Phenomenology*. A. Hofstadter (Trans.). Bloomington, IN: Indiana University Press.

Bibliography & Further Readings

_____. (1990). *Kant and the Problem of Metaphysics*. R. Taft (Trans.). Bloomington, IN: Indiana University Press.

_____. (1994). *Basic Questions of Philosophy*. A. Schuwer (Trans.). Bloomington, IN: Indiana University Press.

_____. (1997). *Phenomenological Interpretation of Kant's Critique of Pure Reason*. P. Emad and K. Maly (Trans.). Bloomington, IN: Indiana University Press.

_____. (1998). *Basic Concepts*. G. E. Aylesworth (Trans.). Bloomington, IN: Indiana University Press.

_____. (2003). *The Heidegger-Jaspers Correspondence (1920-1963)* W. Biemal (Ed.). and Gary E. Aylesworth (Trans.). New York: Humanity Books.

_____. (2005). "Husserl's mangling of phenomenological findings [sic] through the care, derived from Descartes, about certainty." D.O. Dahlstrom (Trans.). In *Introduction to Phenomenological Research*. Bloomington, IN: Indiana University Press.

_____. (2006). "Letter on 'Humanism' (1946)." W. McNeil (Trans.). *Pathmarks*. (pp. 239-277). Cambridge, England: Cambridge University Press.

_____. (2012). *Four Seminars*. A. Mitchell and F. Raffoul (Trans.). Bloomington, IN: Indiana University Press.

_____. (2018). *The Question Concerning the Thing: On Kant's Doctrine of the Transcendental Principles*. J. D. Reid & B. D. Crowe (Trans.). London: Rowman & Littlefield.

Herbert, Daniel. (2016). Kant and Sartre on Temporality. In S. Baiasu (Ed). *Comparing Kant and Sartre*. (pp. 45-61). London: Palgrave Macmillan.

Hölderlin, Friedrich. (1980). *Poems & Fragments*. M. Hamburger (Trans.). Cambridge, England: Cambridge University.

_____. (2003). "Oldest Programme for a System of German Idealism." In J.M. Bernstein (Ed.). *Classic and Romantic German Aesthetics*. (pp. 185-187). Cambridge: University of Cambridge Press.

Hori, Victor Sōgen. (2003). *Zen Sand: The book of capping phrases for Kōan practice*. Honolulu, HI: The University Press of Hawaii.

Husserl, Edmund. (1969). *Formal and Transcendental Logic*. D. Cairns (Trans.). The Hague, Netherlands: Nijhoff.

_____. (1970). *The Crisis of the European Sciences and Transcendental Philosophy: An Introduction to Phenomenological Philosophy*. D. Carr (Trans.). Evanston, IL: Northwestern University Press.

_____. (1982). *Ideas Pertaining to a Pure Phenomenology and to a Phenomenological Philosophy* F. Kersten (Trans.). The Hague, Netherlands: Nijhoff.

_____. (1988). *Cartesian Meditations*. D. Cairns (Trans.). Dordrecht, Netherlands: Kluwer.

_____. (1997). *Psychological and Transcendental Phenomenology and the Confrontation with Heidegger (1927–1931): The Encyclopedia Britannica Article, The Amsterdam Lectures, "Phenomenology and Anthropology" and Husserl's Marginal Notes in Being and Time and Kant and the Problem of Metaphysics*. T. Sheehan & R.T. Palmer (Trans.). *Husserliana: Edmund Husserl – Collected Works, vol. 6*. J. Jansen (Ed.). Dordrecht, Netherlands: Springer.

_____. (2008). *Introduction to Logic and Theory of Knowledge*. C.O. Hill (Trans.). Dordrecht, Netherlands: Springer.

Hyppolite, Jean. (1955) "A Chronology of French Existentialism," *Yale French Studies* 16: 100-102.

_____. (1997). *Logic and Existence*. L. Lawlor and A. Sen (Trans.). Albany: SUNY Press.

Inazō, Nitobe. (1908). *Bushido – The Soul of Japan*. Tokyo, Japan: Teibi Publishing Company.

Inwood, Michael. (1999). *A Heidegger Dictionary*. Oxford, England: Blackwell.

Izenberg, Gerald N. (1976). *The Existentialist Critique of Freud: The Crisis of Autonomy*. Princeton, NJ: Princeton University Press.

Jaspers, Karl. (1995). *Philosophy of Existence*. R. F. Grabau (Trans.). Philadelphia, PA: University of Pennsylvania.

Joseph, Felicity and Jack Reynolds. (2011). Existentialism, Phenomenology and Philosophical Method. In F. Joseph, J. Reynolds & A. Woodward (Eds.), *Continuum Companion to Existentialism*. (pp. 15-36). London: Bloomsbury.

Jung, Carl G. (1971). *Psychological Types*. R. F. C. Hull (Trans.). In H. Read et al. (Series Eds.), *The collected works of C.G. Jung*, Vol. 6. Princeton, NJ: Princeton University Press.

Kant, Immanuel. (1960). *Religion Within the Limits of Reason Alone*. T. M. Greene and H. H. Hudson (Trans.). New York: Harper & Row.

_____. (1992). "Attempt to Introduce the Concept of Negative Magnitudes into Philosophy." *Theoretical Philosophy, 1755-1770*. D. Walford and R. Meerbote (Trans.). Cambridge: University of Cambridge Press.

_____. (1997). *Lectures on Metaphysics*. K. Ameriks and S. Naragon (Trans.). Cambridge: University of Cambridge Press.

_____. (1998). *Critique of Pure Reason*. P. Guyer and A.W. Wood (Trans.). Cambridge: University of Cambridge Press.

_____. (1999). *Critique of Practical Reason*. M. Gregor. (Trans.). Cambridge: University of Cambridge Press.

_____. (2002). *Groundwork of the Metaphysics of Morals*. M. Gregor. (Trans.). Cambridge: University of Cambridge Press.

_____. (2006). *Critique of the Power of Judgment*. P. Guyer and E. Matthews (Trans.). Cambridge: University of Cambridge.

_____. (2017). *The Metaphysics of Morals*. M. Gregor (Trans.). Cambridge, England: Cambridge University Press.

Kellenberger, James. (1997) *Kierkegaard and Nietzsche: Faith and Eternal Acceptance*. London: Palgrave Macmillan.

Bibliography & Further Readings

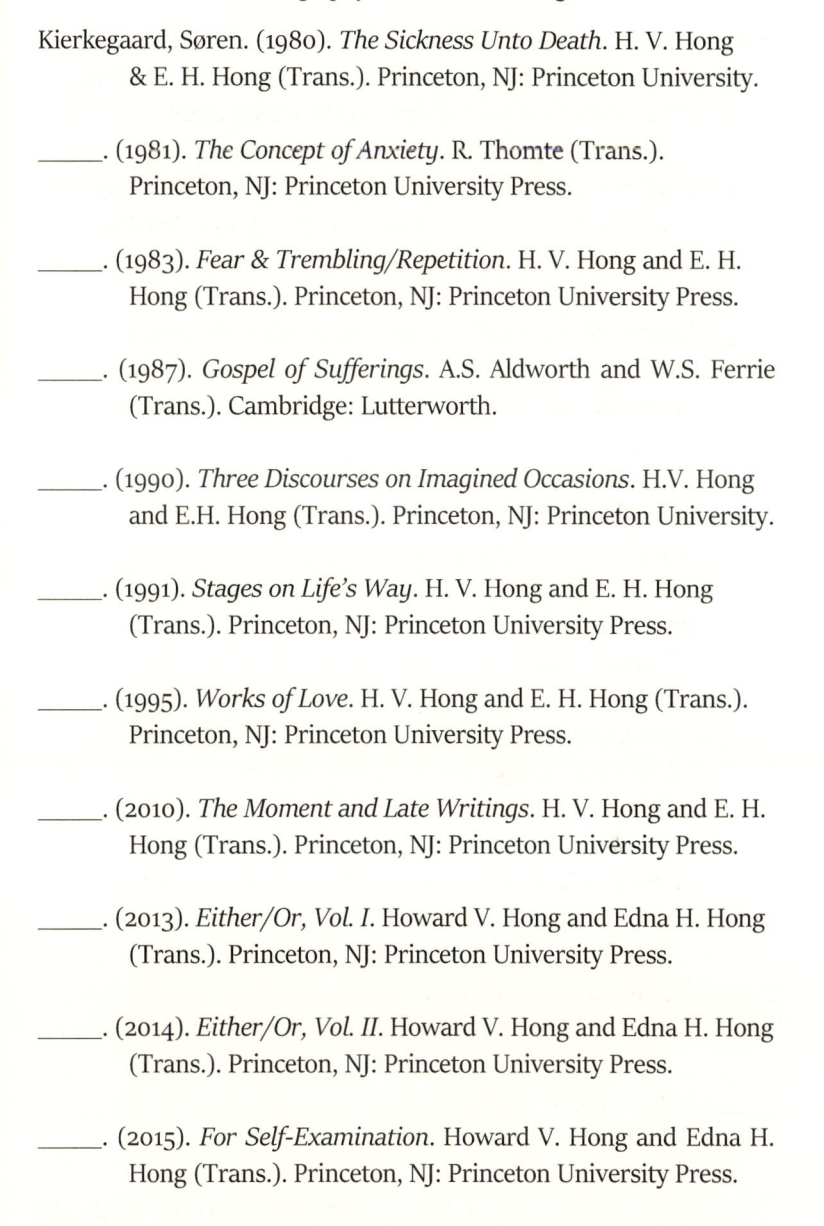

Kierkegaard, Søren. (1980). *The Sickness Unto Death*. H. V. Hong & E. H. Hong (Trans.). Princeton, NJ: Princeton University.

_____. (1981). *The Concept of Anxiety*. R. Thomte (Trans.). Princeton, NJ: Princeton University Press.

_____. (1983). *Fear & Trembling/Repetition*. H. V. Hong and E. H. Hong (Trans.). Princeton, NJ: Princeton University Press.

_____. (1987). *Gospel of Sufferings*. A.S. Aldworth and W.S. Ferrie (Trans.). Cambridge: Lutterworth.

_____. (1990). *Three Discourses on Imagined Occasions*. H.V. Hong and E.H. Hong (Trans.). Princeton, NJ: Princeton University.

_____. (1991). *Stages on Life's Way*. H. V. Hong and E. H. Hong (Trans.). Princeton, NJ: Princeton University Press.

_____. (1995). *Works of Love*. H. V. Hong and E. H. Hong (Trans.). Princeton, NJ: Princeton University Press.

_____. (2010). *The Moment and Late Writings*. H. V. Hong and E. H. Hong (Trans.). Princeton, NJ: Princeton University Press.

_____. (2013). *Either/Or, Vol. I*. Howard V. Hong and Edna H. Hong (Trans.). Princeton, NJ: Princeton University Press.

_____. (2014). *Either/Or, Vol. II*. Howard V. Hong and Edna H. Hong (Trans.). Princeton, NJ: Princeton University Press.

_____. (2015). *For Self-Examination*. Howard V. Hong and Edna H. Hong (Trans.). Princeton, NJ: Princeton University Press.

Kosch, Michelle. (2006). *Freedom and Reason in Kant, Schelling, and Kierkegaard.* Oxford: Oxford University Press.

Kruks, Sonia. (1999). "Gabriel Marcel." In H. Gordon (Ed.), *Dictionary of Existentialism.* Westport, CT: Greenwood Press.

Leland, Dorothy. (2004). The Sartrean Cogito: A Journey between Versions. In C. Guignon, *The Existentialists: Critical Essays on Kierkegaard, Nietzsche, Heidegger, and Sartre.* (pp. 153-164). London: Rowman & Littlefield.

Liezi. (1990). *The Book of Lieh-Tzu: A Classic of the Tao.* A.C. Graham (Trans.). Columbia University Press.

Macquarrie, John. (1968). *Martin Heidegger.* Richmond, VA: John Knox Press.

Marcel, Gabriel. (1949). *Being and Having.* K. Farrer (Trans.), London: Dacre Press.

_____. (1950). *The Mystery of Being, Volume I: Reflection and Mystery (Gifford Lectures, 1949-1950).* G. S. Fraser (Trans.). Chicago, IL: Regnery Company.

_____. (1951). *The Mystery of Being, Volume II: Faith and Reality (Gifford Lectures, 1949-1950).* G. S. Fraser (Trans.). Chicago, IL: Regnery Company.

_____. (1962). *Man Against Mass Society.* G. Fraser (Trans.). Chicago: Henry Regnery Co.

_____. (1963). *The Existential Background of Human Dignity.* Cambridge, MA: Harvard University Press.

———. (1964). "Some Reflections on Existentialism," *Philosophy Today* 8(4): 248-257.

———. (1965). *"Truth and Freedom," Philosophy Today 9(4): 227-237.*

———. (1967). *Presence & Immortality.* M. Machado and H. Koren (Trans.). Pittsburgh, PA: Duquesne University Press.

———. (1968). *Problematic Man.* B. Thompson (Trans.). New York: Herder & Herder.

———. (1973). *Tragic Wisdom and Beyond.* S. Jolin and P. McCormick (Trans.). Evanston, IL: Northwestern University Press.

———. (2001). *Creative Fidelity.* R. Rosthal (Trans.). New York: Fordham University Press.

———. (2002). *The Philosophy of Existentialism.* New York: Citadel.

———. (2009). *Awakenings: A Translation of Marcel's Autobiography.* P.S. Rogers (Trans.). Madison, WI: Marquette University Press.

———. (2010). *Homo Viator: Introduction to the Metaphysic of Hope.* E. Craufurd & P. Seaton (Trans.). South Bend, IN: St. Augustine's Press.

Makkreel, Rudolf. (1984). "Imagination and Temporality in Kant's Theory of the Sublime," *The Journal of Aesthetics and Art Criticism* 42(3): 303-315.

Merleau-Ponty, Maurice. (1964). *Sense & Nonsense*. H. L. Dreyfus & P.A. Dreyfus (Trans.). Evanston, IL: Northwestern University Press.

_____. (2007). *The Merleau-Ponty Reader*. T. Toadvine and L. Lawlor (Eds.) Evanston, IL: Northwestern University Press.

_____. (2012). *Phenomenology of Perception*. D. A. Landes (Trans.). London: Routledge.

Moran, Dermot. (2007). Heidegger's Transcendental Phenomenology in the Light of Husserl's Project of First Philosophy. In S. Crowell and J. Malpas (Eds.). *Transcendental Heidegger*. (pp. 215-234). Stanford, CA: Stanford University Press.

Mounk, Yascha. (2018). "What an Audacious Hoax Reveals About Academia," *The Atlantic* Oct. 5.

Muraton, Mélissa Fox. (2020). Existential Ethics and Liberal Eugenics. *Kierkegaard and Issues in Contemporary Ethics*. (pp. 215-234). Berlin: De Gruyter.

Nabokov, Vladimir. (1949). "Sartre's First Try," *New York Times* Apr. 24.

Nassar, Dalia. (2014). *The Romantic Absolute: Being and Knowing in Early German Romantic Philosophy, 1795-1804*. Chicago, IL: University of Chicago Press.

Niederhauser, Johannes A. (2021). *Heidegger on Death and Being: An Answer to the* Seinsfrage. New York: Springer.

Bibliography & Further Readings

Nietzsche, Friedrich. (1989). *Beyond Good & Evil: Prelude to a Philosophy of the Future*. W. Kaufmann (Trans.). New York: Vintage Books.

_____. (1924). *The Joyful Wisdom*. T. Common (Trans.). London: Allen & Unwin.

_____. (1961). *Thus Spoke Zarathustra: A Book for Everyone and No One*. R.J. Hollingdale (Trans.). Middlesex, England: Penguin Books.

_____. (1967). *The Birth of Tragedy*. W. Kaufmann (Trans.). New York: Vintage Books.

_____. (1968). *Twilight of the Idols/The Anti-Christ*. R.J. Hollingdale (Trans.). Middlesex, England: Penguin.

_____. (1969). *The Will to Power*. W. Kaufmann and R.J. Hollingdale (Trans.). New York: Vintage Books.

_____. (1974). *The Gay Science*. W. Kaufmann. (Trans.). New York: Vintage Books.

_____. (1979). *On Truth and Lies in a Nonmoral Sense*. In *Philosophy and Truth: Selections from Nietzsche's Notebooks of the Early 1870s*, Daniel Breazeale (Ed. and Trans). Hoboken, NJ: Humanities Press.

Nishitani, Keiji. (1995). The Japanese Art of Arranged Flowers. J. Shore (Trans.). In R. C. Solomon and K. M. Higgins (Eds.), *World Philosophy: A Text with Readings*. New York, NY: McGraw Hill.

Norman, Judith. (2002). "Nietzsche and Early Romanticism." *Journal of the History of Ideas* 63(3): 501-519.

Novalis. (1997). *Philosophical Writings*. Albany, NY: SUNY.

Olson, Robert G. (1962). *An Introduction to Existentialism*. New York, NY: Dover Publications.

O'Meara, Thomas F. (1982). *Romantic Idealism and Roman Catholicism: Schelling and the Theologians*. South Bend, IN: University of Notre Dame Press.

Ouden, Bernard D. (1982). *Essays on Reason, Will, Creativity, and Time: Studies in the Philosophy of Friedrich Nietzsche*. Washington, DC: University of Press America.

Pope Pius XII. (1950). "Humanis Generis - Encyclical Letter, Pius XII." *Vatican: The Holy See*. Vatican Website: http://www.vatican.va/content/pius-xii/en/encyclicals/documents/hf_p-xii_enc_12081950_humani-generis.html. Retrieved 02/21/2021.

Quist, Wenche M. (2005). "Nietzsche and Kierkegaard: Tracing Common Themes." *Nietzsche-Studien* 34(1): 474-485.

Raffoul, François. (1998). *Heidegger and the Subject*. D. Pettigrew and G. Recco (Trans.). Hoboken, NJ: Humanities Press.

Richardson, John. (1986). *Existential Epistemology: A Heideggerian Critique of the Cartesian Project*. Oxford, England: Clarendon Press.

Richardson, William J. (2003). *Heidegger: Through Phenomenology to Thought*. New York: Fordham University Press.

Rilke, Rainer Maria. (2020). Orpheus, Eurydice, Hermes. F. Scalambrino (Trans.). In F. Scalambrino (Ed.). *Said It Aloud And Heard It Die Away*. Castalia, OH: Magister Ludi Press.

Rockmore, Tom. (2011). *Kant & Phenomenology*. Chicago, IL: The University of Chicago Press.

Rose, H.J. (1943). "The Grief of Persephone," *The Harvard Theological Review* 36(3): 247-250.

Ruck, Carl A. P. (1981). "Mushrooms and Philosophers." *Journal of Ethnopharmacology* 4(2): 179-205.

Sartre, Jean-Paul. (1964). *Nausea*. L. Alexander (Trans.). New York: New Directions.

_____. (1989). *No Exit and Three Other Plays*. S. Gilbert (Trans.). New York: Vintage.

_____. (1991). *Notebooks for an Ethics*. D. Pellauer (Trans.). Chicago, IL: Chicago University Press.

_____. (1992). *Being and Nothingness: A Phenomenological Essay on Ontology*. H. E. Barnes (Trans.). London: Washington Square Press.

_____. (2000). *Essays in Existentialism*. J. Wahl (Trans.). New York: Citadel Press.

_____. (2001). *What is Literature?* B. Frechtman (Trans.). London: Routledge.

_____. (2004). *The Transcendence of the Ego*. A. Brown (Trans.). London: Routledge.

Scalambrino, Frank. (2003). Thus Spoke Sigmund Freud? *Psychotherapy: Speaking Philosophically.* (pp. 32-40). MA Thesis.

_____. (2011). "Priming effects of the sensory manifold as evidence to solve the Methodological Puzzle regarding accessibility beyond phenomenology," *International Interdisciplinary "Think Art" Conference,* Boston University, October, 2011. Currently unpublished paper. (Forthcoming).

_____. (2013). Invited Review of *Introduction to Philosophy – Thinking and Poetizing* by Martin Heidegger *Philosophy in Review,* XXXIII (4): 294-296.

_____. (2014). "From a phenomenology of the reciprocal nature of habits and values to an understanding of the intersubjective ground of normative social reality." *Phenomenology and Mind* 6: 156-167.

_____. (2015). Phenomenological Psychology, *Internet Encyclopedia of Philosophy.* http://www.iep.utm.edu/phen-psy/. Retrieved 02/20/2021.

_____. (2015). The Temporality of Damnation. In R. Arp and B. McCraw, (Eds.). *The Concept of Hell.* (pp. 66-82). New York: Palgrave.

_____. (2016). 19th Century Existentialism: The Individual & the Mystery of Life. *Introduction to Ethics: A Primer for the Western Tradition.* Dubuque, IA: Kendall Hunt.

_____. (2016). The Shadow of the Sickness Unto Death. In K. S. Decker, et al. (Eds.). *Breaking Bad and Philosophy.* (pp. 47-62). New York: Palgrave.

_____. (2017). *Geisteswissenschaften*. In B. Turner, C. Kyung-Sup, C. Epstein, P. Kivisto, J.M. Ryan & W. Outhwaite (Eds.). *The Wiley-Blackwell Encyclopedia of Social Theory, Vol. II*. 1st Edition. (pp. 912-3). London: Wiley-Blackwell.

_____. (2017). *Living in the Light of Death: Existential Philosophy in the Eastern Tradition, Zen, Samurai & Haiku*. Castalia, OH: Magister Ludi Press.

_____. (2018). *Philosophical Principles of the History and Systems of Psychology: Essential Distinctions*. London: Palgrave.

_____. (2018). Subjectivist Fallacy. In Michael Bruce, et al. (Eds.). *Bad Arguments: 100 of the Most Important Fallacies in Western Philosophy*. (pp. 396-398). London: Wiley-Blackwell.

_____. (2018). "Nietzsche: Spirituality and the Divine." In D. Leeming, (Ed). *Encyclopedia of Psychology & Religion*, 3rd Edition, (pp. 1595-1602). New York: Springer.

_____. (2019). *Full Throttle Heart: The Rapture & Ecstasy of Nietzsche's Dionysian Worldview*. Castalia, OH: Magister Ludi Press.

_____. (2020a). Ambivalence and the Borderline Position in the Existential-Phenomenology of Merleau-Ponty: Being and Having a Body-in-the-World from Primal Ambivalence to Intersubjective Ambiguity. In B. Brogaard and D.E. Gatzia, (Eds.). *The Philosophy and Psychology of Ambivalence*, (pp. 304-321). London: Routledge.

_____. (2020b). Being in the Continental Tradition: Phenomenological Hermeneutics as Fundamental Ontology. In Li Vecchi, Scalambrino, and Kovacs. *The Philosophy of Being in the Analytic, Continental, and Thomistic Traditions*, (pp. 39-82). London: Bloomsbury.

_____. (In Press, 2022). Rhythmic Chaos: The Time Sig-n-ature of Ecstatic Spirit. In I. Joon and J. Weidenbaum, (Eds.). *The Mind in Nature: Extensions of Ecstatic Naturalism*, (pp. TBD). Albany, NY: SUNY Press.

Schaberg, William H. (1995). *The Nietzsche Canon: A Publication History and Bibliography*. Chicago, IL: The University of Chicago Press.

Schact, Richard. (2012). Nietzsche: after the dead of God. In S. Crowell (Ed.). *The Cambridge Companion to Existentialism*. (pp. 111-136). Cambridge, England: Cambridge University Press.

_____. (2013). "Translating Nietzsche: The Case of Kaufmann." *Journal of Nietzsche Studies* 43(1): 66-86.

Schelling, F.W.J. (1980). "Philosophical Letters on Dogmatism and Criticism." *The Unconditional in Human Knowledge: Four Early Essays, 1794-1796*. F. Marti (Trans.). Lewisburg, PA: Bucknell University Press.

_____. (1989). *Ideas for a Philosophy of Nature*. E.E. Harris (Trans.). Cambridge: Cambridge University Press.

_____. (1994). *On the History of Modern Philosophy*. A. Bowie (Trans.). Cambridge, England: Cambridge University Press.

_____. (2003). *Philosophical Inquiries into the Nature of Human Freedom*. J. Gutmann (Trans.). Chicago, IL: Open Court.

_____. (2008). "Timaeus [Commentary]." A. Arola, J. Jolissaint, and P. Warnek (Trans.). *Epoché* 12(2): 205-248.

_____. (2012). *The Grounding of Positive Philosophy: The Berlin Lectures*. B. Matthews (Trans.). Albany, NY: SUNY Press.

_____. (2019). *On the Divinities of Samothrace*. F. Scalambrino (Trans.). Castalia, OH: Magister Ludi Press.

Schopenhauer, Arthur. (1969). *The World as Will and Representation*. Vol. 1. E.F.J. Payne. (Trans.). New York: Dover Publications.

_____. (2001). *Parerga and Paralipomena, Vol. II*. E.F.J. Payne (Trans.). Oxford, England: Oxford University Press.

_____. (2005). *Philosophical Writings*. W. Schirmacher (Trans.). New York: Continuum.

_____. (2020). *On Philosophy at the Universities*. F. Scalambrino (Trans.). Castalia, OH: Magister Ludi Press.

Schwarz, Mary Francesca. (2020). *Marcel's Metaphysics of Hospitality*. [Doctoral Dissertation]. Irving, Texas: University of Dallas.

Shew, Melissa. (2013). "The *Kairos* of Philosophy." *The Journal of Speculative Philosophy* 27(1): 47-66.

Shigesuke, Taira. (1999). *Code of the Samurai*. T. Cleary, (Trans.). Boston, MA: Tuttle Publishing.

Smith, David Woodruff. (2018). "Phenomenology," *The Stanford Encyclopedia of Philosophy*. Edward N. Zalta (Ed.), URL = <https://plato.stanford.edu/archives/sum2018/entries/phenomenology/>. Retrieved 02/01/2021.

Soll, Ivan. (2012). Schopenhauer on the Inevitability of Unhappiness. In B. Vandenabeele (Ed.). *A Companion to Schopenhauer*. (pp. 300-313). Hoboken, NJ: Wiley-Blackwell.

Solomon, Robert C. (1989). *From Hegel to Existentialism*. Oxford, England: Oxford University Press.

_____. (2001). *From Rationalism to Existentialism: The Existentialists and Their Nineteenth-Century Backgrounds*. Boulder, CO: Rowman & Littlefield.

Spiegelberg, Herbert. (1960). "Husserl's Phenomenology and Existentialism," *The Journal of Philosophy* 57 (2): 62-74.

Stewart, Jon. (2010). *Idealism and Existentialism: Hegel and Nineteenth- and Twentieth-Century European Philosophy*. London: Continuum.

Stokes, Patrick and Adam J. Buben (eds), (2011). *Kierkegaard and Death*. Bloomington, IN: Indiana Press.

Stone, Brad Elliott. (2006). "Curiosity as the Thief of Wonder: An Essay on Heidegger's Critique of the Ordinary Conception of Time," *KronoScope* 6(2): 205-229.

Bibliography & Further Readings

Suzuki, Shunryu. (2011). *Zen Mind, Beginner's Mind*. Boston, MA: Shambhala.

Taminiaux, Jacques. (1991). *Heidegger and the Project of Fundamental Ontology*. M. Gendre (Trans.). Albany, NY: SUNY Press.

Thiel, Udo. (2015). *The Early Modern Subject: Self-Consciousness and Personal Identity from Descartes to Hume*. Oxford: Oxford University Press.

de Unamuno, Miguel. (1954). *The Tragic Sense of Life*. J.E. Crawford (Trans.), New York: Dover.

Wahl, Jean. (2019). *Philosophies of Existence: An Introduction to the Basic Thought of Kierkegaard, Heidegger, Jaspers, Marcel, Sartre*. New York: Routledge.

Warnock, Mary. (2019). *The Philosophy of Sartre*. London: Routledge.

Werkmeister, W. H. (1941). "An Introduction to Heidegger's 'Existential Philosophy,'" *Philosophy and Phenomenological Research* 2 (1): 79-87.

White, Alan. (1983). *Schelling: An Introduction to the System of Freedom*. New Haven, CT: Yale University Press.

Willcutt, Zachary. (2020). "Marcel and Augustine on Immortality: The Nothingness of the Self and the Exteriorization of Love as the Way to Eternity." *Marcel Studies* 5(1): 1-18.

Wong, Kwok Kui. (2010). "Schelling's Criticism of Kant's Theory of Time." *Idealistic Studies* 40(1): 83-102.

Wood, Allen. (2007). *Kantian Ethics*. Cambridge, England: Cambridge University Press.

Wood, Robert E. (2005). Introduction. In G. Marcel (Auth). *Music and Philosophy*. S. Maddux and R.E. Wood (Trans.). (pp. 11-40). Milwaukee, WI: Marquette University Press.

Woodward, F.L. (1922). The Ethics of Suicide in Greek, Latin and Buddhist Literature. *Buddhist Annual of Ceylon* Vol. 4 Colombo, Ceylon: W.E. Bastian & Co.

Zanetti, Luca. (2020). "Why Am I Here? The Challenges of Exploring Children's Existential Questions in the Community of Inquiry." *Childhood and Philosophy* 16(36): 1-26.

Ziolkowski, Theodore. (1990). *German Romanticism and Its Institutions*. Princeton, NJ: Princeton University Press.

Index for Volumes I & II

Abbagnano, Nicola
  VII 58
Abyss
  VI 69, 72, 74-6;
  VII 53, 57-8, 63
Adorno, Theodor W.
  VII 135-7
Alienation
  VI 43-8, 51, 112, 133-4, 150; **VII** 45
Amor Fati
  VI 42, 51-4, 56-8, 83, 87-8, 90, 98, 105, fn.115, 141;
  VII 70, 79, 82, 105
Anxiety
  VI 14, 37-9, 42, 59, 64, 73-8, 87, 90, 104, 107-8, 111-5, 131, 137, 148-9;
  VII xi-i, 46-7, 52-6, 62-3, 69, 73-4, 76, 79, 84, 99-105, 117, 142-3, 150, 153, 155, 159, 165
Apotheosis
  VI 42, 45-6, 50-2, 54, 58, 87, 90, 99;
  VII 32, 45, 49, 56, 58, 105, 159-60, 163
Aristotle
  VI 5, 20, 36; **VII** 30
Atheism
  VI 4, 60;
  VII 20, 23, 39-40, 43, 121
Authenticity
  VI 14, 37-9, 42, 47-8, 58-9, 62-4, 70-3, 77-9, 87, 90-5, 98-9, 101-2, 104-5, 107, 109--119, 131, 135-8, 140-9, 152, 154;

Authenticity (cont.)
  VII 33, 36, 46-52, 55, 59, 66, 82, 84, 88, 92, 96, 102-5, 109, 126-33, 135, 137, 142-3, 149-55, 159, 164
Bad Faith
  VI 58, 77, 80, 134, 137, 140;
  VII 31, 33, 40, 47-8, 51, 55
de Beauvoir, Simone
  VI 7;
  VII 19, 27
Camus, Albert
  VII 138-9
Commitment
  VI 14, 38-9, 64, 81, 138, 146-7, 149; **VII** 38, 71, 77, 84, 88-90, 94, 128, 159, 165
Consciousness
  VI 14, 17, 20-34, 38, 42-4, 47-9, 51, 56, 58, 72, 81, 92-4, 96-8, fn. 100, 119-124, 126, 132-7, 144-5, 153;
  VII 22-3, 26-8, 32, 34, 114-5, 118-119, 149, 159
Conscience
  VI 14, 38, 64, 76, 90-1, 107, 111, 114-5;
  VII 47, 55, 76, 97-8, fn. 100, 150, 152-9
Contexts (Thematic Genera) for Determining & Understanding the Meaning of Life
  VI 34-9, 64, 85, 90, 94, 107, 150-1;
  VII 18, 30-33, 36-7, 44, 47, 51, 54, 63, 71, 81, 91-2, 96, fn. 100, 114, 145, 152

Death
  VI 1, 9, 14, 37-9, 42, 48, 62-66, 73, 77-82, 94, 98-106, 108-9, 111-2, 115-8, 141-2, 144, 152;
  VII xi, xiv, 56-7, 63, 65, 74, 77, 79-85, 87-90, 95, 97-8, 100-5, 109, 133, 138, 150, 153-5, 159, 162-3
Deleuze, Gilles
  VI 90-1, 111; **VII** 136
Descartes, René
  VI 5, 57, 65, 100-1, 119, 123, 125-6, 133-5, 139; **VII** x, 18, 24-30, 47, 109, 118
Dreyfus, Hubert
  VI fn. 2
Engels, Friedrich
  VI 66
Eternal Return
  VI 82-4, 87-92, 98-9; **VII** 52, 70, 79
Eternity
  VI 48, 58, 71, 124, 146; **VII** 57, 66-9, 79
Existence Precedes Essence
  VII 19-5, 39-40, 109, 126
Fate (incl. Destiny & Vocation)
  VI 21, 37, 57-8, 66, 70-2, 86, 89, 90, 92, 112;
  VII x, xii, 82, 87, 91-98, 104-6, 127-8
Fichte, J.G.
  VI 66
Fidelity
  VI 138-9, 141-2, 145-8, 151-4;
  VII 58
Frankl, Viktor
  VI fn. 70

Freedom
  VI 1, 14, 26, 32, 34-35, 38, 42, 48, 51, 59, 64, 70, 72, 74-8, 81, 84, 87, 92, 99, 104-9, 111, 113, 119, 131, 134, 137-9, 146, 148-9, 152-3;
  VII xiii, xiv, 46-9, 52-9, 64, fn. 65-6, 69, 72, 74, 76, 82, 89-94, 97-99, 101-5, 140-44, 151, 154, 159-64
Feuerbach, Ludwig
  VI 66
Friedrich, Caspar David
  VI 41, 46
German Romanticism
  VI 6, 10-11, 41, 43, 46-8, 51-3, 71, 95;
  VII 31, 104, 108, 160
Guilt
  VI fn. 64, 74, 76, 107, 111-5;
  VII 76, 82, 97-8, 125, 153
Hedonism
  VI 79; **VII** 143, 149-53
Hegel, GWF
  VI 11, 41, 60-2, 65-6, 68, 71-2, 81, 119-21, 142;
  VII 34, 42, 108, 135, 137-8
Heidegger, Martin
  VI 1-2, 5-8, 20, 35-7, 51, 61-5, 69, 71, 75-77, 79, fn. 87-8, 98-118, 120, 125, 127, 130, 140, 143-5, 147, 149-52;
  VII x-xi, xiv, 17, 21-4, 26, 28, 31-4, 36-8, 41, 47-50, 52-53, 55, 57, 59-60, 63, 65, 71, 74, 77, 79-80, 82-3, 89-91, 95-8, 108, 115, 117-121, 126-128, 133, 135-7, 143-4, 149-55, 162-3, 165

The Herd
  VI 49, 56, 77, 89, 93-4;
  VII 32, 44, 47, 50
Historie
  VI 62-3, 69; **VII** 73
Hölderlin, Friedrich
  VI 10, 48; **VII** xi
Humanism
  VI 2; **VII** xiii, 18-19, 24,
  26-7, 34, 39, 41-5, 109, 140
Husserl, Edmund
  VI fn. 2, fn. 100, 120, 122,
  132-5; **VII** 25-6, 28, 34, 36,
  115-121, 125
Individuation/Individuated Be-ing
  VI 23-4, 31-2, 42-3, 46-8, 52,
  58, 71, 75-77, 81, 85, 108-9,
  112-3, 126, 151;
  VII 23, 25, 33-8, 68, 84, 106,
  153, 164-6
Integrity
  VI 14, 38-9, 42, 59, 64, 70,
  72, 78-9, 81, 87, 90-2, 94-5,
  98-99, 105, 114-7, 131, 135-
  8, 141, 143, 146-8, fn. 151,
  154; **VII** 46, 66, 85, 87, 89-
  90, 96, 102-5, 132
Jung, Carl G
  VII 164-6
Kant, Immanuel
  VI 5, 7-14, 17-42, 44, 49, 53,
  60-3, 65-6, 68-9, 71, 73, 75-6,
  84-6, 93, 100-1, 107, 109,
  111, 120-1, 123, 127, 129,
  136, fn. 151, 152;
  VII 18, 27-34, 36, 39-40, fn.
  47, 50, 55, 57-67, 70, 77, 79-
  81, 91, 108, 113-6, 118-121,
  125, 129, 137, 149, fn. 150,
  159

Keats, John
  VI 50
Kierkegaard, Søren
  VI 1, 4, 7, 22, 37, 59, 61-2,
  64-6, 68, 73-81, 83-4, 98,
  103-4, 107, 118, 120, 123,
  140, 146-7, 150;
  VII xi-iii, 24, 26, 31, 36, 39,
  47, 50, 52-7, 60, 66-71, 77,
  79-80, 82-84, 88-9, 108, 115-
  6, 121, 143-4
Leibniz, G.W.
  VI 26; **VII** 29
Leypold, Julius von
  VI 41, 46-7
Locke, John
  VI 26; **VII** 29
Marcel, Gabriel
  VI 6-7, 138-154;
  VII 19, 39-40, 58, 108, 125
Marx, Karl
  VI 66, 120;
  VII 41-5, 130-1, 133, 137
Meaning-Making
  VI 14, 24, 34-6, 38-9, 42, 44-
  6, 58, 63, 94, 129-32, 136-8,
  142-4, 150; **VII** 18, 35-6, 40,
  fn. 59, 90-2, 94-8, 100-1, 129,
  131, 140, 142-8, 159, 161-4
Merleau-Ponty, Maurice
  VI 136; **VII** 19, 101, 125
Mineness
  VI 14, 24-7, 32-4, 36-9, 41,
  47, 52, 59, 71-2, 76, 78-9, 84,
  87, 92, 99, 104-111, 113,
  116-7, 119, 128, 131, 136-
  143, 146-8, 153-4;
  VII 25, 28, 46, 49, 51, 54-6,
  58, 70-1, 76, 82-4, 89-95, 98-
  102, 105, 131, 143-7, 149-64

(the) Moment of Vision
>**VI** 45, 59; **VII** xiv, 17, 59-80, 84, 88, 90, 95, 98-99, 101-2, 105-6, 109, 127-9, 144, 152, 154-5

Mystery
>**VI** 14, 21, 26, 34, 38, 41-3, 52, 59, 72, 80, 84-7, 92, 97, 105-6, 108-9, 111-3, 115, 121, 130-1, 138-141, 144-6, 149, 153;
>**VII** 46, 90-3, 99, 101-2, 159-61

Nietzsche, Friedrich
>**VI** 1, 7, 10, 37, 41, 45, 47, 51-8, 62, 68-71, 76-7, 81-99, 103, 105, 107, 111, fn. 115, 118, 120, 123, 140, 145, 150-2; **VII** xii-xiii, 31-32, 39, 47, 50, 52-3, 58-60, 70, 77, 79-80, 82, 90, 108, 115-7, 121

Nihilism
>**VI** 48, 55, 60-5, 72, 81, 97, 142-3, 146, 149;
>**VII** 31, fn. 66, 108

Novalis
>**VI** 10, 41, 45-6, 48, 51, 87; **VII** xii, 32, 87

Phenomenology
>**VI** 9, 71, 120, 122, 132;
>**VII** 17, 26, 34, fn. 100, 105, 113-6, 118-20, 136-7, 149

(the) Person/Personal/Personhood
>**VI** 36, 38, 47, 49, 64, 72, 76-81, 58, 93-4, 99, 109, 123, 138-9, 142, 149, 151-2;
>**VII** 20, 30-3, 37-8, 45, 48-50, 52-3, 58, 81, 83, 91, 95, 105-6, 140-4, 153

Plato
>**VI** 14, 20, 36, 38, 43, 48-49; **VII** 30, 80,117

Pope Pius XII
>**VI** 125

Principles of Existentialism
>**VI** 13-4, 17-8, 26, 34, 36-9, 42, 59, 62, 66, 68, 72-3, 75, 81, 84, 87, 92, 100, 103, 105, 110, 114-5, 118-121, 125, 130-2, 137-8, 141, 145-6, 148, 153-4;
>**VII** 18, 46-7, 66, 87-8, 94, 101-3, 107-9, 140-1, 159-65

(Existence as a) Quest
>**VI** 42, fn. 45, 51-8, 82-3, 90-2, 149; **VII** 84, 141, 159

Resoluteness
>**VI** 14, 38-9, 98, 111, 114-7, 137, 144-5, 147;
>**VII** xiv, 73-6, 80, 83-5, 95, 97, 102, 130, 155, 159

Rogers, Carl (Person-Centered Psychotherapy)
>**VII** 140-145

Sartre, Jean-Paul
>**VI** 1-2, 4-8, 37, 61, 64, 71, 77, 103, 118-38, 140, 145-7, 149;
>**VII** xii-xiii, 19-29, 31, 33-4, 39-41, 44-8, 52-3, 55, 57, fn. 59, 108, 120-1, 125-9, 131, 134, 139

Schelling, FWJ
>**VI** 10-11, 45, 48, 59, 61, 65-73, 75, 87;
>**VII** x-xi, 26, fn. 60

Scala Amoris
>**VI** 14, 38, 48, 50-1;
>**VII** 159

Schopenhauer, Arthur
    VI 10-11, 48, 61, 65-72, 75, 82, 87, fn. 127;
    VII xii, 117, 133, 135

Sincerity
    VI 14, 38-9, 42, 59, 64, 70, 72, 78-81, 87, 90-1, 94-6, 98-9, 105, 115-6, 132, 137, 141, 143, 146-8, 154;
    VII 46, 66, 90, 96, 102-5, 132-3, 142, 159-164

Spinoza, Benedict
    VI 60

(the) Subject/Subjectivity
    VI 5, 22, 27-9, 36, 44, 54, 79, 81, 95-6, 98, 119-122, 133-9, 151-3;
    VII 18, 20-8, 33-8, 41, 43, 47, 49-50, 62, 64, fn. 65, 82, 118, 136

(the) Sublime
    VI 21, 50, 52, 97;
    VII 62-5, 79, 81, 85

Transcendental Unity of Apperception
    VI 23, 25-8, 31-7, 127, 136;
    VII 29-30, 47, 49, 63-4, 91, 98, 118-9, 159-160, 163-4

Temporality
    VI 9, 24, 71, 103, 117, 143, 146-7;

Temporality (cont.)
    VII xiv, 38, 66, 68-73, 76, 80, 83, 102, 137, 143, 149, 152, 154-5

The They (the Nobody)
    VI 111-3, 149;
    VII 32, 49, 50-1, 53, fn. 59, 72, 76, 92, 98, 132, 155

Thrownness
    VI 99, 102, 107-8, 112-7, 119, 126; **VII** xi, xiii-xiv, 73, 75-6, 83, 90-99, 101, 103-4, 106, 128, 154-5, 165

Transcendental Philosophy
    VI 7-10, 13-4, 17-20, 25-6, 35-6, 46, 51, 53-4, 60, 62, 65, 69, 73, 84, 100;
    VII 35, 44, 47, 52, 57, 59-62, 70, 108, 116, 121, 125, 149

Utilitarianism
    VII 45-6

Worldliness
    VI 14, 37-8, 47, 71, 73, 76-7, 79-81, 99, 104-7, 110-13, 116, 127, 137-40, 142, 148, 153;
    VII 25, 31, 33, 51, 54-6, 63, 68, 70-1, 83-4, 89-91, 94, 100, 106, 129, 153, 159-163

ABOUT THE AUTHOR

This is Frank Scalambrino's ninth book; additionally, he has produced one edited volume and one anthology, authored over fifty professional peer-reviewed publications, and taught over one hundred university-level courses, including graduate-level courses in both philosophy and psychology.

His podcast "Basic Philosophical Questions," "Philosopheme" videos, and full courses are presently being made available to the public.

His translations include passages from the dialogues of Plato and lectures, essays, letters, and poems by Schelling, Schopenhauer, Nietzsche, and Rilke.

He is the first person in the history of Western philosophy to explicitly solve "the problem of 'non-being'" as evidenced by his Doctoral Dissertation: *Non-Being & Memory: A Critique of Pure Difference*.

Before age 27 he founded a Community Mental Health Suicide Prevention Respite Unit and Clinical Intervention Center; he subsequently received awards from multiple mental health agencies across the local, county, and state levels of Ohio, and, in the same year, was inducted into Chi Sigma Iota, the international counseling honor society.

In determining his projects as an author, he believes: "Empty is the word of that philosopher by whom no affliction of men is cured. For as there is no benefit in medicine if it does not treat the diseases of the body, so with philosophy, if it does not drive out the affliction of the soul." ~Epicurus, "Fragment #54."

Made in the USA
Monee, IL
22 August 2021